# The Complete
# Murphy's
# Law

## A Definitive Collection

Arthur Bloch

PRICE STERN SLOAN

Los Angeles

Cover illustration by Rick Penn-Kraus
Interior illustrations by Ed Powers

Text copyright © 1991, 1990, 1984, 1982, 1977 by Arthur Bloch

Illustrations copyright © 1991, 1990 by Price Stern Sloan, Inc.

Published by Price Stern Sloan, Inc.
11150 Olympic Boulevard, Suite 650
Los Angeles, California 90064

Printed in the United States of America.

10 9 8 7 6 5 4 3 2

This book has been printed on acid-free paper.

ISBN: 0-8431-2824-0

# ACKNOWLEDGMENTS AND PERMISSIONS

Grateful acknowledgment is made to the following for permission to reprint their material:

"Datamation." *Laws of Computer Programming*. Greenwich, Connecticut: Technical Publishing Co., 1968.

"Spark's Ten Rules for the Project Manager"; "Laws of Procrastination"; "Gordon's First Law"; "Maier's Law"; "Edington's Theory"; "Parkinson's Law for Medical Research"; "Peter's Hidden Postulate According to Godin"; "Godin's Law"; "Freeman's Rule"; "Old and Kahn's Law"; "First Law of Socio-Genetics"; "Hersh's Law." *Journal of Irreproducible Results*. Box 234, Chicago Heights, Illinois.

Parkinson, C. Northcote. "Parkinson's First, Second, Third, Fourth and Fifth Laws", "Parkinson's Law of Delay"; "Parkinson's Axioms." *Parkinson's Law, Mrs. Parkinson's Law, The Law and the Profits, The Law of Delay* and *In-Laws and Outlaws*. Boston: Houghton Mifflin Company.

Peter, Dr. Laurence J. and Raymond Hull. "The Peter Principle and Its Corollaries: Peter's Inversion; Peter's Placebo; Peter's Prognosis; Peter's Law of Evolution*; Peter's Observation*; Peter's Law of Substitution*; Peter's Rule for Creative Incompetence*; Peter's Theorem.*" *The Peter Principle*. New York: William Morrow and Co., 1969.
(*so named by the editors)

"Matz's Laws, Mottos, etc."; "Barach's Rule"; "Bernstein's Precept"; "Cochrane's Aphorism"; "Lord Cohen's Comment"; "Loeb's Laws of Medicine"; "Shumway's Law." *New York State Journal of Medicine,* copyright by the Medical Society of the State of New York, "Principles of Medicine," (Jan. 1977) and "More Principles of Medicine," (Oct. 1977) by Robert Matz, M.D.

Shedenhelm, W.R.C. "Shedenhelm's Laws of Backpacking." *The Backpacker's Guide*. Mountain View: World Publications, 1979.

Block, Herbert, "Herblock's Law." *Herblock's State of the Union*. New York: Simon & Schuster, 1972.

Alinsky, Saul. "Alinsky's Rule for Radicals." *Rules for Radicals*. New York: Random House, Inc., 1971.

"Kamin's Law." *L.A. Herald Examiner*. Dec. 2, 1973.

"Glogg's Law." *National Review*. (150 East 35th St., New York, NY, 10016), Mar. 29, 1974.

Bloch, Arthur. "Four Workshop Principles"; "Five Laws of Office Murphology"; "Eight Laws of Kitchen Confusion"; "Laws of Class Scheduling"; "Laws of Applied Terror." *Murphy's Law(s) Plaques for the Workshop; for the Office; for the Kitchen; for Students.* Los Angeles: Price Stern Sloan, Inc., 1978.

"Borkowski's Law"; "Hart's Law of Observation"; "Law of Probable Dispersal." *Verbatim.* 1977.

Gall, John, M.D. "Systematics." *How Systems Work and Especially How They Fail.* New York: Times Books, 1977.

"Hofstedt's Law"; "Horngren's Observation"; "MacDonald's First and Second Laws." *Alumni Bulletin.* Stanford School of Business, Vol. 46, No. 3. Copyright 1978 by the Board of Trustees of Leland Stanford Junior University. All rights reserved.

"Ballance's Law of Relativity"; "Ballance's Law of Pragmatic Passion." *Bill Balance's Hip Handbook of Nifty Moves.* North Hollywood, California: Melvin Powers-Wilshire Book Co.

Reed, Fred. "The Guppy Law." *The Washington Post.* June 27, 1978.

Price, Roger. "Price's Laws." *The Great Roob Revolution.* New York: Random House, Inc., 1970.

"Telesco's Laws of Nursing." *American Journal of Nursing.* Dec. 1978, Vol. 78, No. 12.

"Thumb's First and Second Postulates." *Nuclear News.* Aug. 1971.

Hammond, Alice. "Laws of the Kitchen"; "Working Cooks Laws"; "Cooper's Rule for Copying Recipes." *Randolph Guide* and *Greensboro Record.* Mar. 8, 1978.

"Law of Revelation"; "Evans' Law." *Dukengineer.* October, 1974.

Murray, Jim. "Murray's Rules of the Arena." *L.A. Times.* Nov. 23, 1978.

Smith, Jack. "Dedera's Law." *L.A. Times.* Nov. 10, 1976.

"Byrne's Law of Concreting." *Western Construction.* May 1978.

"Golomb's Don'ts of Mathematical Modeling." *Astronautics and Aeronautics.* American Institute of Astronautics and Aeronautics. January 1968.

"Finnigan's Law." *Organic Gardening.* June 1978.

Fox, Joe. "Disraeli's Dictum"; "Wilkie's Law"; "Things That Can Be Counted on in a Crisis." *Trapped in the Organization.* Los Angeles: Price Stern Sloan, Inc., 1980.

"The Lippman Lemma." *The Worm Runner's Digest.* Vol. 21, No. 1. 1979.

Lowe, Frances. "Lowe's Law." *Lubbock Avalanche-Journal.* January 28, 1979.

Macbeth's Comment on Evolution: "Towards," 17417 Vintage St., Northridge, CA, 91325, Vol. 2, No. 2.

Caen, Herb. "Olivier's Law," "Cooger's Law," *San Francisco Chronicle.* Nov. 29, 1981.

Roche, John P. "Roche's Fifth Law." *Albany Times-Union.* July 14, 1978.

Schrank, Robert. "Schrank's First Law." *Ten Thousand Working Days.* Cambridge, MA: MIT Press, 1978.

Very special thanks also to Conrad Schneiker for his invaluable assistance and support.

# TABLE OF CONTENTS

# INTRODUCTION

Have you ever received a phone call the minute you sat down on the toilet? Has the bus you were waiting for ever appeared the instant you lit up a cigarette? Has it ever rained the day you washed your car, or stopped raining just after you bought an umbrella? Perhaps you realized at the time that something was afoot, that some universal principle was just out of your grasp, itching to be called by name. Or perhaps, having heard of Murphy's Law, the Peter Principle or the Law of Selective Gravity, you have wanted to invoke one of these, only to find that you have forgotten its exact wording.

Here, then, is the first complete reference book of the wit and wisdom of our most delightfully demented technologists, bureaucrats, humanists and antisocial observers, prepared and presented with the purpose of providing us all with a little Karmic Relief. The listing has been made as definitive as possible. In researching these interdisciplinary tenets, we found numerous redundancies (which verify the validity of the observations), frequent conflicting claims to authorship and scores of anonymous donations. We are forced to acknowledge the contribution of the inimitable Zymurgy who said, "Once you open a can of worms, the only way to recan them is to use a larger can." By applying this Murphic morsel to the present volume, we come to realize that this project, once undertaken, has grown in size and scope as further principles, new and old, have been revealed by our beacon of truth.

Throughout history pundits and poseurs have regaled us with the laws of the universe, the subtle yet immutable substructure that is the basis of cosmic order. From people of religion we have received the Moral Laws; from mystics, the Laws of Karma; from rationalists, the Laws of Logical Form; and from artists, the Laws of Aesthetics. Now it is the technologists' turn to bend our collective ear.

The official party line of technology, of science itself, is despair. If you doubt this, witness the laws of thermodynamics as they are restated in Ginsberg's Theorem: 1. You can't win; 2. You can't break even; 3. You can't even quit the game. The universe is simmering down, like a giant stew left to cook for four billion years. Sooner or later we won't be able to tell the carrots from the onions.

"But what of the short run, the proverbial closed system?" you may well ask as you sit gazing out of your penthouse window, sipping your vodka martini and watching the hustling throngs of God's little creatures going about their business. Alas, we've only to look at this business, as exemplified in the good bureaucracy, through the eyes of Peter, Parkinson, et al. We will realize that it is only a matter of time before the microcosmic specks we call big business and government, like their universal counterpart, lose their ability to succeed in spite of themselves.

"We are on the wrong side of the tapestry," said Father Brown, G. K. Chesterton's famous clerical sleuth. And indeed we are. A few loose ends, an occasional thread, are all we ever see of the great celestial masterwork of the most expensive carpet weaver of them all. A small number of courageous individuals have dared to explore the far side of the tapestry, have braved the wrath of the Keeper of the Rug in their search for truth. It is to these individuals that this volume is dedicated.

# MURPHOLOGY

## MURPHY'S LAW:

If anything can go wrong, it will.

## Corollaries:

1. Nothing is as easy as it looks.
2. Everything takes longer than you think.
3. If there is a possibility of several things going wrong, the one that will cause the most damage will be the one to go wrong.
4. If you perceive that there are four possible ways in which a procedure can go wrong, and circumvent these, then a fifth way will promptly develop.
5. Left to themselves, things tend to go from bad to worse.
6. Whenever you set out to do something, something else must be done first.
7. Every solution breeds new problems.
8. It is impossible to make anything foolproof because fools are so ingenious.
9. Mother nature is a bitch.

## BENEDICT'S PRINCIPLE
## (formerly Murphy's Ninth Corollary):

Nature always sides with the hidden flaw.

## LAW OF REVELATION:

The hidden flaw never remains hidden.

## THE MURPHY PHILOSOPHY:

Smile. Tomorrow will be worse.

## MURPHY'S CONSTANT:

Matter will be damaged in direct proportion to its value.

## QUANTIZATION REVISION .
## OF MURPHY'S LAW:

1. If we lose much by having things go wrong, take all possible care.
2. If we have nothing to lose by change, relax.
3. If we have everything to gain by change, relax.
4. If it doesn't matter, it does not matter.

## LOFTA'S LAMENT:

Nobody can leave well enough alone.

## O'TOOLE'S COMMENTARY ON MURPHY'S LAW:

Murphy was an optimist.

## ZYMURGY'S SEVENTH EXCEPTION TO MURPHY'S LAW:

When it rains, it pours.

## BOLING'S POSTULATE:

If you're feeling good, don't worry. You'll get over it.

## CHRIS' COMMENT:

You always have to give up something you want for something you want more.

## WHITE'S STATEMENT:

Don't lose heart.

### Owen's Commentary on White's Statement:

They might want to cut it out.

### Byrd's Addition to Owen's Commentary on White's Statement:

And they want to avoid a lengthy search.

## ILES' LAW:

There is always an easier way to do it.

## Corollaries:

1. When looking directly at the easier way, especially for long periods, you will not see it.
2. Neither will Iles.

## HEYMANN'S LAW:

Mediocrity imitates.

## CHISHOLM'S FIRST LAW:

When things are going well, something will go wrong.

## Corollaries:

1. When things just can't get any worse, they will.
2. Anytime things appear to be going better, you have overlooked something.

## CHISHOLM'S SECOND LAW:

Proposals, as understood by the proposer, will be judged otherwise by others.

## Corollaries:

1. If you explain something so clearly that nobody can misunderstand, somebody will.

2. If you do something which you are sure will meet with everybody's approval, somebody won't like it.

3. Procedures devised to implement the purpose won't quite work.

## LAW OF THE LIE:

No matter how often a lie is shown to be false, there will remain a percentage of people who believe it true.

## SCOTT'S FIRST LAW:

No matter what goes wrong, it will probably look right.

## SCOTT'S SECOND LAW:

When an error has been detected and corrected, it will be found to have been correct in the first place.

### Corollary:

After the correction has been found in error, it will be impossible to fit the original quantity back into the equation.

## GUMPERSON'S LAW:

The probability of anything happening is in inverse ratio to its desirability.

## ISSAWI'S LAWS OF PROGRESS:

The Course of Progress:
Most things get steadily worse.

The Path of Progress:
A shortcut is the longest distance between two points.

The Dialectics of Progress:
Direct action produces direct reaction.

The Pace of Progress:
Society is a mule, not a car. If pressed too hard, it will kick and throw off its rider.

## SODD'S FIRST LAW:

When a person attempts a task, he or she will be thwarted in that task by the unconscious intervention of some other presence (animate or inanimate). Nevertheless, some tasks are completed, since the intervening presence is itself attempting a task and is, of course, subject to interference.

## SODD'S SECOND LAW:

Sooner or later, the worse possible set of circumstances is bound to occur.

### Corollary:

Any system must be designed to withstand the worst possible set of circumstances.

## SIMON'S LAW:

Everything put together falls apart sooner or later.

## GEORGE'S LAW:
All pluses have their minuses.

## ARISTOTLE'S DICTUM:
One should always prefer the probable impossible to the improbable possible.

## RUDIN'S LAW:
In crises that force people to choose among alternative courses of action, most people will choose the worst one possible.

## GINSBERG'S THEOREM:
1. You can't win.
2. You can't break even.
3. You can't even quit the game.

## FREEMAN'S COMMENTARY ON GINSBERG'S THEOREM:
Every major philosophy that attempts to make life seem meaningful is based on the negation of one part of Ginsberg's Theorem. To wit:
1. Capitalism is based on the assumption that you can win.
2. Socialism is based on the assumption that you can break even.

3. Mysticism is based on the assumption that you can quit the game.

## EHRMAN'S COMMENTARY:
1. Things will get worse before they get better.
2. Who said things would get better?

## EVERITT'S LAW OF THERMODYNAMICS:
Confusion is always increasing in society. Only if someone or something works extremely hard can this confusion be reduced to order in a limited region. Nevertheless, this effort will still result in an increase in the total confusion of society at large.

## BOBBY'S BELIEF:
Confusion not only reigns, it pours.

## MURPHY'S LAW OF THERMODYNAMICS:
Things get worse under pressure.

## LUNSFORD'S RULE OF SCIENTIFIC ENDEAVOR:
The simple explanation always follows the complex solution.

## RUDNICKI'S NOBEL PRINCIPLE:

Only someone who understands something absolutely can explain it so no one else can understand it.

## COMMONER'S LAW OF ECOLOGY:

Nothing ever goes away.

## PUDDER'S LAW:

Anything that begins well, ends badly.
Anything that begins badly, ends worse.

## STOCKMAYER'S THEOREM:

If it looks easy, it's tough.
If it looks tough, it's damn well impossible.

## WYNNE'S LAW:

Negative slack tends to increase.

## TYLCZAK'S PROBABILITY POSTULATE:

Random events tend to occur in groups.

## ZYMURGY'S LAW OF EVOLVING SYSTEMS DYNAMICS:

Once you open a can of worms, the only way to recan them is to use a larger can.

## KAISER'S COMMENT ON ZYMURGY:

Never open a can of worms unless you plan to go fishing.

## STURGEON'S LAW:

Ninety percent of everything is crud.

## NON-RECIPROCAL LAWS OF EXPECTATIONS:

Negative expectations yield negative results.
Positive expectations yield negative results.

## LAW OF REGRESSIVE ACHIEVEMENT:

Last year's was always better.

## THE UNSPEAKABLE LAW:

As soon as you mention something
— if it's good, it goes away.
— if it's bad, it happens.

# APPLIED
# MURPHOLOGY

## BOOKER'S LAW:

An ounce of application is worth a ton of abstraction.

## KLIPSTEIN'S LAWS:

Applied to General Engineering:

1. A patent application will be preceded by a similar application submitted one week earlier by an independent worker.
2. Firmness of delivery dates is inversely proportional to the tightness of the schedule.
3. Dimensions will always be expressed in the least usable term. Velocity, for example, will be expressed in furlongs per fortnight.
4. Any wire cut to length will be too short.

Applied to Prototyping and Production:

1. Tolerances will accumulate unidirectionally toward maximum difficulty to assemble.
2. If a project requires "n" components, there will be "n-1" units in stock.
3. A motor will rotate in the wrong direction.
4. A fail-safe circuit will destroy others.
5. A transistor protected by a fast-acting fuse will protect the fuse by blowing first.

6. A failure will not appear until a unit has passed final inspection.

7. A purchased component or instrument will meet its specs long enough, and only long enough, to pass incoming inspection.

8. After the last of sixteen mounting screws has been removed from an access cover, it will be discovered that the wrong access cover has been removed.

9. After an access cover has been secured by sixteen hold-down screws, it will be discovered that the gasket has been omitted.

10. After an instrument has been assembled, extra components will be found on the bench.

## PATTISON'S LAW OF ELECTRONICS:

If wires can be connected in two different ways, the first way blows the fuse.

## FARRELL'S LAW OF NEWFANGLED GADGETRY:

The most expensive component is the one that breaks.

# THE RECOMMENDED PRACTICES COMMITTEE OF THE INTERNATIONAL SOCIETY OF PHILOSOPHICAL ENGINEERS' UNIVERSAL LAWS FOR NAIVE ENGINEERS:

1. In any calculation, any error that can creep in will do so.
2. Any error in any calculation will be in the direction of most harm.
3. In any formula, constants (especially those obtained from engineering handbooks) arc to be treated as variables
4. The best approximation of service conditions in the laboratory will not begin to meet those conditions encountered in actual service.
5. The most vital dimension on any plan or drawing stands the greatest chance of being omitted.
6. If only one bid can be secured on any project, the price will be unreasonable.
7. If a test installation functions perfectly, all subsequent production units will malfunction.
8. All delivery promises must be multiplied by a factor of 2.0.

9. Major changes in construction will always be requested after fabrication is nearly completed.

10. Parts that positively cannot be assembled in improper order will be.

11. Interchangeable parts won't.

12. Manufacturer's specifications of performance should be multiplied by a factor of 0.5.

13. Salespeople's claims for performance should be multiplied by a factor of 0.25.

14. Installation and Operating Instructions shipped with the device will be promptly discarded by the Receiving Department.

15. Any device requiring service or adjustment will be least accessible.

16. Service Conditions as given on specifications will be exceeded.

17. If more than one person is responsible for a miscalculation, no one will be at fault.

18. Identical units that test in an identical fashion will not behave in an identical fashion in the field.

19. If, in engineering practice, a safety factor is set through service experience at an ultimate value, an ingenious idiot will promptly calculate a method to exceed said safety factor.

20. Warranty and guarantee clauses are voided by payment of the invoice.

## HARPER'S MAGAZINE LAW:

You never find an article until you replace it.

## RICHARD'S COMPLEMENTARY RULES OF OWNERSHIP:

1. If you keep anything long enough you can throw it away.
2. If you throw anything away, you will need it as soon as it is no longer accessible.

## GILLETTE'S LAW OF HOUSEHOLD MOVING:

What you lost during your first move you find during your second move.

## HEISENBERG'S UNCERTAINTY PRINCIPLE:

The location of all objects cannot be known simultaneously.

### Corollary:

If a lost thing is found, something else will disappear.

## O'BRIEN'S OBSERVATION:

The quickest way to find something is to start looking for something else.

## MARYANN'S LAW:

You can always find what you're not looking for.

## ADVANCED LAW OF THE SEARCH:

The first place to look for anything is the last place you would expect to find it.

## BOOB'S LAW:

You always find something in the last place you look.

## BLOCH'S REBUTTAL TO BOOB'S LAW

You always find something in the first place you look, but you never find it the first time you look there.

## GLATUM'S LAW OF MATERIALISTIC ACQUISITIVENESS:

The perceived usefulness of an article is inversely proportional to its actual usefulness once bought and paid for.

## GILLETTE'S LAW OF TELEPHONE DYNAMICS:

The phone call you've been waiting for comes the minute you're out the door.

## FRANK'S PHONE PHENOMENA:

If you have a pen, there's no paper.

If you have paper, there's no pen.

If you have both, there's no message.

## WOLTER'S LAW:

If you have the time, you won't have the money.

If you have the money, you won't have the time.

# ADVANCED MURPHOLOGY

## SCHNATTERLY'S SUMMING UP
## OF THE COROLLARIES:

If anything can't go wrong, it will.

## SILVERMAN'S PARADOX:

If Murphy's Law can go wrong, it will.

## THE EXTENDED MURPHY'S LAW:

If a series of events goes wrong, it will do so in
the worst possible sequence.

## FARNSDICK'S COROLLARY
## TO THE FIFTH COROLLARY:

After things have gone from bad to worse, the
cycle will repeat itself.

## GATTUSO'S EXTENSION
## OF MURPHY'S LAW:

Nothing is ever so bad that it can't get worse.

## NAGLER'S COMMENT ON
## THE ORIGIN OF MURPHY'S LAW:

Murphy's Law was not propounded by Murphy,
but by another man of the same name.

## LYNCH'S LAW:

When the going gets tough, everyone leaves.

## KOHN'S COROLLARY
## TO MURPHY'S LAW:

Two wrongs are only the beginning.

## McDONALD'S COROLLARY
## TO MURPHY'S LAW:

In any given set of circumstances, the proper course of action is determined by subsequent events.

## MURPHY'S LAW OF GOVERNMENT:

If anything can go wrong, it will do so in triplicate.

## MAAHS' LAW:

Things go right so they can go wrong.

## ADDENDUM TO MURPHY'S LAW:

In precise mathematical terms, $1 + 1 = 2$, where "=" is a symbol meaning "seldom if ever."

## GUALTIERI'S LAW OF INERTIA:

Where there's a will, there's a won't.

## MURPHY'S UNCERTAINTY PRINCIPLE:

You can know something has gone wrong only when you make an odd number of mistakes.

## TUSSMAN'S LAW:

Nothing is as inevitable as a mistake whose time has come.

## LAW OF PROBABLE DISPERSAL:

Whatever hits the fan will not be evenly distributed.

## FAHNSTOCK'S RULE FOR FAILURE:

If at first you don't succeed, destroy all evidence that you tried.

## EVANS' AND BJORN'S LAW:

No matter what goes wrong, there is always somebody who knew it would.

## LANGSAM'S LAWS:

1. Everything depends.
2. Nothing is always.
3. Everything is sometimes.

## HELLRUNG'S LAW:

If you wait, it will go away.

## Shavelson's Extension:

Having done its damage.

## Grelb's Addition:

If it was bad, it'll be back.

## GROSSMAN'S MISQUOTE OF H.L. MENCKEN:

Complex problems have simple, easy-to-understand wrong answers.

## DUCHARME'S PRECEPT:

Opportunity always knocks at the least opportune moment.

## FLUGG'S LAW:

When you need to knock on wood is when you realize the world is composed of aluminum and vinyl.

## IMBESI'S LAW OF THE CONSERVATION OF FILTH:

In order for something to become clean, something else must become dirty.

## Freeman's Extension:
But you can get everything dirty without getting anything clean.

## FIRST POSTULATE OF ISO-MURPHISM:
Things equal to nothing else are equal to each other.

## RUNE'S RULE:
If you don't care where you are, you ain't lost.

## COIT-MURPHY'S STATEMENT ON THE POWER OF NEGATIVE THINKING:
It is impossible for an optimist to be pleasantly surprised.

## FERGUSON'S PRECEPT:
A crisis is when you can't say, "Let's forget the whole thing."

## THE UNAPPLICABLE LAW:
Washing your car to make it rain doesn't work.

## MURPHY'S SAVING GRACE:
The worst is enemy of the bad.

## THE CARDINAL CONUNDRUM:

An optimist believes we live in the best of all possible worlds. A pessimist fears this is true.

## NAESER'S LAW:

You can make it foolproof, but you can't make it damnfoolproof.

## DUDE'S LAW DUALITY:

Of two possible events, only the undesired one will occur.

## HANE'S LAW:

There is no limit to how bad things can get.

## PERRUSSEL'S LAW:

There is no job so simple that it cannot be done wrong.

## MAE WEST'S OBSERVATION:

To err is human, but it feels divine.

## THINE'S LAW:

Nature abhors people.

## BORKOWSKI'S LAW:

You can't guard against the arbitrary.

## LACKLAND'S LAWS:

1. Never be first.
2. Never be last.
3. Never volunteer for anything.

## HIGDON'S LAW:

Good judgment comes from bad experience.
Experience comes from bad judgment.

## THE PAROUZZI PRINCIPLE:

Given a bad start, trouble will increase at an
exponential rate.

## THE CHI FACTOR:

Quantity = $\dfrac{1}{\text{Quality}}$ ; or, quantity is inversely
proportional to quality.

## LAW OF PARTICULATE ATTRACTION:

A flying particle will seek the nearest eye.

## MESKIMEN'S LAW:

There's never time to do it right, but there's
always time to do it over.

## SCHOPENHAUER'S LAW OF ENTROPY:

If you put a spoonful of wine in a barrel full of sewage, you get sewage.

If you put a spoonful of sewage in a barrel full of wine, you get sewage.

## ALLEN'S LAW:

Almost anything is easier to get into than to get out of.

## FROTHINGHAM'S LAW:

Urgency varies inversely with importance.

## THE ROCKEFELLER PRINCIPLE:

Never do anything you wouldn't be caught dead doing.

## YOUNG'S LAW OF INANIMATE MOBILITY:

All inanimate objects can move just enough to get in your way.

## LAW OF THE PERVERSITY OF NATURE:

You cannot successfully determine beforehand which side of the bread to butter.

## LAW OF SELECTIVE GRAVITY:

An object will fall so as to do the most damage.

## Jenning's Corollary:

The chance of the bread falling with the buttered side down is directly proportional to the cost of the carpet.

## Klipstein's Corollary:

The most delicate component will be the one to drop.

## SPRINKEL'S LAW:

Things always fall at right angles.

## FULTON'S LAW OF GRAVITY:

The effort to catch a falling, breakable object will produce more destruction than if the object had been allowed to fall in the first place.

## PAUL'S LAW:

You can't fall off the floor.

# PROBLEMATICS

## SMITH'S LAW:

No real problem has a solution.

## HOARE'S LAW OF LARGE PROBLEMS:

Inside every large problem is a small problem struggling to get out.

## THE SCHAINKER CONVERSE TO HOARE'S LAW OF LARGE PROBLEMS:

Inside every small problem is a larger problem struggling to get out.

## BIG AL'S LAW:

A good solution can be successfully applied to almost any problem.

## PEER'S LAW:

The solution to a problem changes the nature of the problem.

## BARUCH'S OBSERVATION:

If all you have is a hammer, everything looks like a nail.

## DISRAELI'S DICTUM:

Error is often more earnest than truth.

## FOX ON PROBLEMATICS:

When a problem goes away, the people working to solve it do not.

## WALDROP'S PRINCIPLE:

The person not here is the one working on the problem.

### Corollary:

If the person is not expected back, he is the one responsible for the problem.

## BIONDI'S LAW:

If your project doesn't work, look for the part you didn't think was important.

## VAN GOGH'S LAW:

Whatever plan one makes, there is a hidden difficulty somewhere.

## THE ROMAN RULE:

The one who says it cannot be done should never interrupt the one who is doing it.

## LAW OF THE GREAT IDEA:

The one time you come up with a great solution, somebody else has just solved the problem.

## BLAIR'S OBSERVATION:

The best laid plans of mice and men are usually about equal.

## SEAY'S LAW:

Nothing ever comes out as planned.

## RUCKERT'S LAW:

There is nothing so small that it can't be blown out of proportion.

## VAN HERPEN'S LAW:

The solving of a problem lies in finding the solvers.

## HALL'S LAW:

The means justify the means. The approach to a problem is more important than its solution.

## BAXTER'S LAW:

An error in the premise will appear in the conclusion.

## McGEE'S FIRST LAW:

It's amazing how long it takes to complete something you are not working on.

# BUREAUCRATICS

## THE BUREAUCRACY PRINCIPLE:

Only a bureaucracy can fight a bureaucracy.

## FOX ON BUREAUCRACY:

A bureaucracy can outwait anything.

### Corollary:

Never get caught between two bureaucracies.

## YOUNG'S LAW:

It is the dead wood that holds up the tree.

### Corollary:

Just because it is still standing doesn't mean it is not dead.

## HOFFSTEDT'S EMPLOYMENT PRINCIPLE:

Confusion creates jobs.

## SOPER'S LAW:

Any bureaucracy reorganized to enhance efficiency is immediately indistinguishable from its predecessor.

## GIOIA'S THEORY:

The person with the least expertise has the most opinions.

## OWEN'S THEORY OF ORGANIZATIONAL DEVIANCE:

Every organization has an allotted number of positions to be filled by misfits.

### Corollary:

Once a misfit leaves, another will be recruited.

## POST'S MANAGERIAL OBSERVATION:

The inefficiency and stupidity of the staff corresponds to the inefficiency and stupidity of the management.

## AIGNER'S AXIOM:

No matter how well you perform your job, a superior will seek to modify the results.

## THE PITFALLS OF GENIUS:

No boss will keep an employee who is right all the time.

## MOLLISON'S BUREAUCRACY HYPOTHESIS:

If an idea can survive a bureaucratic review and be implemented, it wasn't worth doing.

## PARKINSON'S FIFTH LAW:
If there is a way to delay an important decision, the good bureaucracy, public or private, will find it.

## PARKINSON'S LAW OF DELAY:
Delay is the deadliest form of denial.

## LOFTUS' THEORY ON PERSONNEL RECRUITMENT:
1. Faraway talent always seems better than home-developed talent.
2. Personnel recruiting is a triumph of hope over experience.

## LOFTUS' LAW OF MANAGEMENT:
Some people manage by the book, even though they don't know who wrote the book or even what the book is.

## JOE'S LAW:
The inside contact that you have developed at great expense is the first person to be let go in any reorganization.

## THE LIPPMAN DILEMMA:
People specialize in their area of greatest weakness.

## THINGS THAT CAN BE COUNTED ON IN A CRISIS:
MARKETING says yes.
FINANCE says no.
LEGAL has to review it.
PERSONNEL is concerned.
PLANNING is frantic.
ENGINEERING is above it all.
MANUFACTURING wants more floor space.
TOP MANAGEMENT wants someone responsible.

## COHN'S LAW:
In any bureaucracy, paperwork increases as you spend more and more time reporting on the less and less you are doing. Stability is achieved when you spend all of your time reporting on the nothing you are doing.

## SWEENEY'S LAW:
The length of a progress report is inversely proportional to the amount of progress.

## MORRIS' LAW OF CONFERENCES:

The most interesting paper will be scheduled simultaneously with the second most interesting paper.

## COLLINS' CONFERENCE PRINCIPLE:

The speaker with the most monotonous voice speaks after the big meal.

## McNAUGHTON'S RULE:

Any argument worth making within the bureaucracy must be capable of being expressed in a simple declarative sentence that is obviously true once stated.

## PATTON'S LAW:

A good plan today is better than a perfect plan tomorrow.

## JACOBSON'S LAW:

The less work an organization produces, the more frequently it reorganizes.

# HIERARCHIOLOGY

## PERKINS' POSTULATE:

The bigger they are, the harder they hit.

## HARRISON'S POSTULATE:

For every action, there is an equal and opposite criticism.

## ROGERS' RULE:

Authorization for a project will be granted only when none of the authorizers can be blamed if the project fails but when all of the authorizers can claim credit if it succeeds.

## GATES' LAW:

The only important information in a hierarchy is who knows what.

## RULE OF DEFACTUALIZATION:

Information deteriorates upward through bureaucracies.

## BACHMAN'S INEVITABILITY THEOREM:

The greater the cost of putting a plan into operation, the less chance there is of abandoning the plan — even if it subsequently becomes irrelevant.

## Corollary:

The higher the level of prestige accorded to the people behind the plan, the less chance there is of abandoning it.

## CONWAY'S LAW:

In any organization there will always be one person who knows what is going on.
This person must be fired.

## FOX ON LEVELOLOGY:

What will get you promoted on one level will get you killed on another.

## STEWART'S LAW OF RETROACTION:

It is easier to get forgiveness than permission.

## FIRST RULE OF SUPERIOR INFERIORITY:

Don't let your superiors know you're better than they are.

## WHISTLER'S LAW:

You never know who's right, but you always know who's in charge.

## SPENCER'S LAWS OF DATA:

1. Anyone can make a decision given enough facts.
2. A good manager can make a decision without enough facts.
3. A perfect manager can operate in perfect ignorance.

## GOTTLIEB'S RULE:

The boss who attempts to impress employees with his or her knowledge of intricate details has lost sight of the final objective.

## DINGLE'S LAW:

When somebody drops something, everybody will kick it around instead of picking it up.

## KUSHNER'S LAW:

The chances of anybody doing anything are inversely proportional to the number of other people who are in a position to do it instead.

## PFEIFER'S PRINCIPLE:

Never make a decision you can get someone else to make.

## Corollary:

No one keeps a record of decisions you could have made but didn't. Everyone keeps a record of your bad ones.

## THAL'S LAW:

For every vision, there is an equal and opposite revision.

## MacDONALD'S LAW:

It's tough to get reallocated when you're the one who's redundant.

## WELLINGTON'S LAW OF COMMAND:

The cream rises to the top.
So does the scum.

## HELLER'S LAW:

The first myth of management is that it exists.

### Johnson's Corollary:

Nobody really knows what is going on anywhere within the organization.

## THE PETER PRINCIPLE:

In a hierarchy, every employee tends to rise to his level of incompetence.

## Corollaries:

1. In time, every post tends to be occupied by an employee who is incompetent to carry out his or her duties.
2. Work is accomplished by those employees who have not yet reached their level of incompetence.

## PETER'S INVERSION:

Internal consistency is valued more highly than efficient service.

## PETER'S HIDDEN POSTULATE ACCORDING TO GODIN:

Every employee begins at his level of competence.

## PETER'S OBSERVATION:

Super-competence is more objectionable than incompetence.

## PETER'S LAW OF EVOLUTION:

Competence always contains the seed of incompetence.

## PETER'S RULE FOR CREATIVE INCOMPETENCE:

Create the impression that you have already reached your level of incompetence.

## PETER'S THEOREM:

Incompetence plus incompetence equals incompetence.

## PETER'S LAW OF SUBSTITUTION:

Look after the molehills and the mountains will look after themselves.

## PETER'S PROGNOSIS:

Spend sufficient time in confirming the need and the need will disappear.

## PETER'S PLACEBO:

An ounce of image is worth a pound of performance.

## GODIN'S LAW:

Generalizedness of incompetence is directly proportional to highestness in hierarchy.

## FREEMAN'S RULE:

Circumstances can force a generalized incompetent to become competent, at least in a specialized field.

## VAIL'S AXIOM:

In any human enterprise, work seeks the lowest hierarchicalal level.

## IMHOFF'S LAW:

The organization of any bureaucracy is very much like a septic tank — the really big chunks always rise to the top.

## PARKINSON'S AXIOMS:

1. An official wants to multiply subordinates, not rivals.
2. Officials make work for each other.

## SOCIOLOGY'S IRON LAW OF OLIGARCHY:

In every organized activity, no matter what the sphere, a small number will become the oligarchical leaders and the others will follow.

## OESER'S LAW:

There is a tendency for the person in the most powerful position in an organization to spend all of his or her time serving on committees and signing letters.

## ZYMURGY'S LAW OF VOLUNTEER LABOR:

People are always available for work in the past tense.

## THE SALARY AXIOM:

The pay raise is just large enough to increase your taxes and just small enough to have no effect on your take-home pay.

## MURPHY'S OBSERVATION ON BUSINESS:

The toughest thing in business is minding your own.

## LAW OF COMMUNICATIONS:

The inevitable result of improved and enlarged communications between different levels in a hierarchy is a vastly increased area of misunderstanding.

## DOW'S LAW:

In a hierarchical organization, the higher the level, the greater the confusion.

## BUNUEL'S LAW:

Overdoing things is harmful in all cases, even when it comes to efficiency.

## SPARK'S TEN RULES FOR THE PROJECT MANAGER:

1. Strive to look tremendously important.
2. Attempt to be seen with important people.
3. Speak with authority; however, only expound on the obvious and proven facts.
4. Don't engage in arguments, but if cornered, ask an irrelevant question and lean back with a satisfied grin while your opponent tries to figure out what's going on — then quickly change the subject.
5. Listen intently while others are arguing the problem. Pounce on a trite statement and bury them with it.
6. If a subordinate asks you a pertinent question, look at him as if he has lost his sense. When he looks down, paraphrase the question back at him.
7. Obtain a brilliant assignment, but keep out of sight and out of the limelight.
8. Walk at a fast pace when out of the office —

this keeps questions from subordinates and
superiors at a minimum.

9. Always keep the office door closed. This puts
   visitors on the defensive and also makes it look
   as if you are always in an important
   conference.
10. Give all orders verbally. Never write anything
    down that might go into a "Pearl Harbor File."

## TRUTHS OF MANAGEMENT:

1. Think before you act; it's not your money.
2. All good management is the expression of one
   great idea.
3. No executive devotes effort to proving himself
   wrong.
4. If sophisticated calculations are needed to
   justify an action, don't do it.

## JAY'S LAW OF LEADERSHIP:

Changing things is central to leadership, and
changing them before anyone else is creativeness.

## MATCH'S MAXIM:

A fool in a high station is like a man on the top of
a high mountain; everything appears small to him
and he appears small to everybody.

## WORKER'S DILEMMA:

1. No matter how much you do, you'll never do enough.
2. What you don't do is always more important than what you do do.

## IRON LAW OF DISTRIBUTION:

Them that has, gets.

## THE ARMY AXIOM:

Any order that can be misunderstood has been misunderstood.

## LAW OF SOCIO-ECONOMICS:

In a hierarchical system, the rate of pay for a given task increases in inverse ratio to the unpleasantness and difficulty of the task.

## PUTT'S LAW:

Technology is dominated by two types of people: Those who understand what they do not manage. Those who manage what they do not understand.

## JONES' LAW:

The man who can smile when things go wrong has thought of someone he can blame it on.

# COMMITTOLOGY

## McKERNAN'S MAXIM:

Those who are unable to learn from past meetings are condemned to repeat them.

## COURTOIS' RULE:

If people listened to themselves more often, they would talk less.

## OLD AND KAHN'S LAW:

The efficiency of a committee meeting is inversely proportional to the number of participants and the time spent on deliberations.

## SHANAHAN'S LAW:

The length of a meeting rises with the square of the number of people present.

## LAW OF TRIVIALITY:

The time spent on any item of the agenda will be in inverse proportion to the sum involved.

## ISSAWI'S LAWS OF COMMITTO-DYNAMICS:

1. *Comitas comitatum, omnia comitas.*
2. The less you enjoy serving on committees, the more likely you will be pressed to do so.

## MATILDA'S LAW OF SUB-COMMITTEE FORMATION:

If you leave the room, you're elected.

## THIRD LAW OF COMMITTO-DYNAMICS:

Those most opposed to serving on committees are made chairpersons.

## MITCHELL'S LAWS OF COMMITTOLOGY:

1. Any simple problem can be made insoluble if enough conferences are held to discuss it.
2. Once the way to screw up a project is presented for consideration it will invariably be accepted as the soundest solution.
3. After the solution screws up the project, all those who initially endorsed it will say, "I wish I had voiced my reservations at the time."

## KIM'S RULE OF COMMITTEES:

If an hour has been spent amending a sentence, someone will move to delete the paragraph.

## THE ELEVENTH COMMANDMENT:

Thou shalt not committee.

## KENNEDY'S COMMENT ON COMMITTEES:

A committee is twelve people doing the work of one.

## KIRBY'S COMMENT ON COMMITTEES:

A committee is the only life form with twelve stomachs and no brain.

## HENDRICKSON'S LAW:

If a problem causes many meetings, the meetings eventually become more important than the problem.

## LORD FALKLAND'S RULE:

When it is not necessary to make a decision, it is necessary not to make a decision.

## FAIRFAX'S LAW:

Any facts which, when included in the argument, give the desired results, are fair facts for the argument.

## HUTCHINS' LAW:

You can't outtalk a man who knows what he's talking about.

## FAHNSTOCK'S LAW OF DEBATE:

Any issue worth debating is worth avoiding altogether.

## HARTZ'S LAW OF RHETORIC:

Any argument carried far enough will end up in semantics.

## GOURD'S AXIOM:

A meeting is an event at which the minutes are kept and the hours are lost.

## FIRST LAW OF BUSINESS MEETINGS:

The lead in a pencil will break in direct proportion to the importance of the notes being taken.

## SECOND LAW OF BUSINESS MEETINGS:

If there are two possible ways to spell a person's name, you will pick the wrong spelling.

## TRUMAN'S LAW:

If you cannot convince them, confuse them.

## FIRST LAW OF DEBATE:

Never argue with a fool — people might not know the difference.

## SWIPPLE'S RULE OF ORDER:

He who shouts loudest has the floor.

## RAYBURN'S RULE:

If you want to get along, go along.

## BOREN'S LAWS:

1. When in doubt, mumble.
2. When in trouble, delegate.
3. When in charge, ponder.

## PARKER'S RULE OF PARLIAMENTARY PROCEDURE:

A motion to adjourn is always in order.

# STATESMANSHIP AND ECONO-MURPHOLOGY

## LIEBERMAN'S LAW:

Everybody lies, but it doesn't matter since nobody listens.

## LAW OF THE LIE:

No matter how often a lie is shown to be false, there will remain a percentage of people who believe it true.

## THE SAUSAGE PRINCIPLE:

People who love sausage and respect the law should never watch either one being made.

## JACQUIN'S POSTULATE ON DEMOCRATIC GOVERNMENT:

No person's life, liberty or property are safe while the legislature is in session.

## TODD'S TWO POLITICAL PRINCIPLES:

1. No matter what they're telling you, they're not telling you the whole truth.
2. No matter what they're talking about, they're talking about money.

## ANDRA'S POLITICAL POSTULATE:

Foundation of a party signals the dissolution of the movement.

## KAMIN'S LAW:

When attempting to predict and forecast macro-economic moves of economic legislation by a politician, never be misled by what he says; instead — watch what he does.

## THE WATERGATE PRINCIPLE:

Government corruption is always reported in the past tense.

## ALINSKY'S RULE FOR RADICALS:

Those who are most moral are farthest from the problem.

## MARX'S RULE OF POLITICS:

As soon as they become rich, they become Republican.

## RULE OF POLITICAL PROMISES:

Truth varies.

## LEE'S LAW:

In any dealings with a collective body of people, the people will always be more tacky than originally expected.

## EVAN'S LAW:

If you can keep your head when all about you are losing theirs, then you just don't understand the problem.

## RUSK'S LAW OF DELEGATION:

Where an exaggerated emphasis is placed upon delegation, responsibility, like sediment, sinks to the bottom.

## THE GUPPY LAW:

When outrageous expenditures are divided finely enough, the public will not have enough stake in any one expenditure to squelch it.

### Corollary:

Enough guppies can eat a treasury.

## WIKER'S LAW:

Government expands to absorb revenue and then some.

## GOOD'S RULE FOR DEALING WITH BUREAUCRACIES:

When the government bureau's remedies do not match your problem, you modify the problem, not the remedy.

## MARKS' LAW OF MONETARY EQUALIZATION:

A fool and your money are soon partners.

## HEISENBERG PRINCIPLE OF INVESTMENT:

You may know where the market is going, but you can't possibly know where it's going after that.

## JEFF'S THEORY OF THE STOCK MARKET:

The price of a stock moves inversely to the number of shares purchased.

## HORNGREN'S OBSERVATION:

Among economists, the real world is often a special case.

## HELGA'S RULE:

Say no, then negotiate.

## GLYME'S FORMULA FOR SUCCESS:

The secret of success is sincerity. Once you can fake that you've got it made.

## O'BRIEN'S LAW:

Nothing is ever done for the right reasons.

## SPENCER'S LAWS OF ACCOUNTANCY:

1. Trial balances don't.
2. Working capital doesn't.
3. Liquidity tends to run out.
4. Return on investments won't.

## PRICE'S LAWS:

1. If everybody doesn't want it, nobody gets it.
2. Mass man must be served by mass means.
3. Everything is contagious.

## BROWN'S RULES OF LEADERSHIP:

1. To succeed in politics, it is often necessary to rise above your principles.
2. The best way to succeed in politics is to find a crowd that's going somewhere and get in front of them.

## THE RULE OF LAW:

If the facts are against you, argue the law.
If the law is against you, argue the facts.
If the facts and the law are against you, yell like hell.

## MILES' LAW:

Where you stand depends on where you sit.

## FIBLEY'S EXTENSION TO MILES' LAW:

Where you sit depends on who you know.

## FOX ON POWER:

Arrogance is too often the companion of excellence.

## WALTON'S LAW OF POLITICS:

A fool and his money are soon elected.

## THE FIFTH RULE OF POLITICS:

When a politician gets an idea, he usually gets it wrong.

## WILKIE'S LAW:

A good slogan can stop analysis for fifty years.

## SHERMAN'S RULE OF PRESS CONFERENCES:

The explanation of a disaster will be made by a stand-in.

## ROCHE'S LAW:

Every American crusade winds up as a racket.

## MILLER'S LAW:

Exceptions prove the rule — and wreck the budget.

## BUCKWALD'S LAW:

As the economy gets better, everything else gets worse.

## OGDEN NASH'S LAW:

Progress may have been all right once, but it went on too long.

## FINNIGAN'S LAW:

The farther away the future is, the better it looks.

## SIMON'S LAW OF DESTINY:

Glory may be fleeting, but obscurity is forever.

## THOMPSON'S THEOREM:

When the going gets weird, the weird turn pro.

## McCLAUGHRY'S LAW OF ZONING:

Where zoning is not needed, it will work perfectly. Where it is desperately needed, it always breaks down.

## MURPHY'S MONETARY MAXIM:

Inflation is never having it so good and parting with it so fast.

# FIRST LAW OF POLITICS:

Stay in with the outs.

# PARKS' LAW OF INSURANCE RATES AND TAXES:

Whatever goes up, stays up.

# FIRST LAW OF MONEY DYNAMICS:

A surprise monetary windfall will be accompanied by an unexpected expense of the same amount.

# ROBBINS' MINI-MAX RULE OF GOVERNMENT:

Any minimum criteria set will be the maximum value used.

# LOWE'S LAW:

Success always occurs in private, and failure in full public view.

# EXPERTSMANSHIP

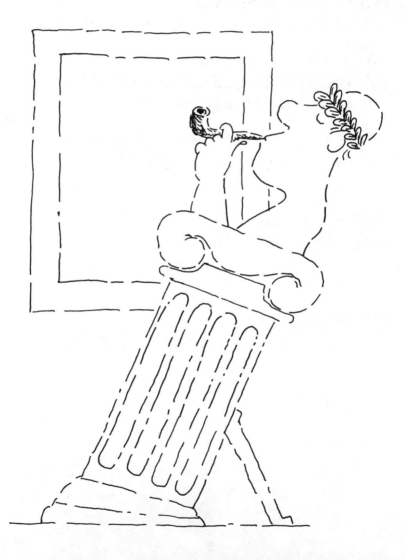

## HOROWITZ'S RULE:

Wisdom consists of knowing when to avoid perfection.

## DE NEVERS' LAW OF COMPLEXITY:

The simplest subjects are the ones you don't know anything about.

## CHRISTIE-DAVIES' THEOREM:

If your facts are wrong but your logic is perfect, then your conclusions are inevitably false. Therefore, by making mistakes in your logic, you have at least a random chance of coming to a correct conclusion.

## McCLELLAN'S LAW OF COGNITION:

Only new categories escape the stereotyped thinking associated with old abstractions.

## HARTZ'S UNCERTAINTY PRINCIPLE:

Ambiguity is invariant.

## DE NEVERS' LAW OF DEBATE:

Two monologues do not make a dialogue.

## EMERSON'S OBSERVATION:

In every work of genius we recognize our rejected thoughts.

## HIRAM'S LAW:

If you consult enough experts you can confirm any opinion.

## JORDAN'S LAW:

An informant who never produces misinformation is too deviant to be trusted.

## DE NEVERS' LOST LAW:

Never speculate on that which can be known for certain.

## LAS VEGAS LAW:

Never bet on a loser because you think his luck is bound to change.

## VAN ROY'S FIRST LAW:

If you can distinguish between good advice and bad advice, then you don't need advice.

## HOWE'S LAW:

Everyone has a scheme that will not work.

## MUNDER'S COROLLARY TO HOWE'S LAW:

Everyone who does not work has a scheme that does.

## FOX ON DECISIVENESS:

1. Decisiveness is not in itself a virtue.
2. To decide not to decide is a decision. To fail to decide is a failure.
3. An important reason for an executive's existence is to make sensible exceptions to policy.

## RULE OF THE OPEN MIND:

People who are resistant to change cannot resist change for the worse.

## ELY'S KEY TO SUCCESS:

Create a need and fill it.

## BRALEK'S RULE FOR SUCCESS:

Trust only those who stand to lose as much as you when things go wrong.

## THE GOLDEN RULE OF ARTS AND SCIENCES:

Whoever has the gold makes the rules.

## GUMMIDGE'S LAW:

The amount of expertise varies in inverse proportion to the number of statements understood by the general public.

## DUNNE'S LAW:

The territory behind rhetoric is too often mined with equivocation.

## MALEK'S LAW:

Any simple idea will be worded in the most complicated way.

## ALLISON'S PRECEPT:

The best simple-minded test of expertise in a particular area is the ability to win money in a series of bets on future occurrences in that area.

## POTTER'S LAW:

The amount of flak received on any subject is inversely proportional to the subject's true value.

## THE RULE OF THE WAY OUT:

Always leave room to add an explanation if it doesn't work out.

## ROSS' LAW:

Never characterize the importance of a statement in advance.

## CLARKE'S FIRST LAW:

When a distinguished but elderly scientist states that something is possible, he is almost certainly right. When he states that something is impossible, he is very probably wrong.

## CLARKE'S SECOND LAW:

The only way to discover the limits of the possible is to go beyond them into the impossible.

## CLARKE'S LAW OF REVOLUTIONARY IDEAS:

Every revolutionary area — in Science, Politics, Art or whatever — evokes three stages of reaction. They may be summed up by the three phrases:
1. "It is impossible — don't waste my time."
2. "It is possible, but it is not worth doing."
3. "I said it was a good idea all along."

## RULE OF THE GREAT:

When somebody you greatly admire and respect appears to be thinking deep thoughts, he or she is probably thinking about lunch.

## CLARKE'S THIRD LAW:

Any sufficiently advanced technology is indistinguishable from magic.

## LAW OF SUPERIORITY:

The first example of superior principle is always inferior to the developed example of inferior principle.

## BLAAUW'S LAW:

Established technology tends to persist in spite of new technology.

## COHEN'S LAW:

What really matters is the name that you are able to impose upon the facts — not the facts themselves.

## FITZ-GIBBON'S LAW:

Creativity varies inversely with the number of cooks involved with the broth.

## BARTH'S DISTINCTION:

There are two types of people: those who divide people into two types, and those who don't.

## SEGAL'S LAW:

A man with one watch knows what time it is.
A man with two watches is never sure.

## MILLER'S LAW:

You can't tell how deep a puddle is until you step in it.

## LaCOMBE'S RULE OF PERCENTAGES:

The incidence of anything worthwhile is either 15-25 percent or 80-90 percent.

### Dudenhoefer's Corollary:

An answer of 50 percent will suffice for the 40-60 range.

## WEILER'S LAW:

Nothing is impossible for the man who doesn't have to do it himself.

## WEINBERG'S FIRST LAW:

If builders built buildings the way programmers wrote programs, then the first woodpecker that came along would destroy civilization.

## WEINBERG'S COROLLARY:

An expert is a person who avoids the small errors while sweeping on to the grand fallacy.

# ADVANCED EXPERTSMANSHIP

## MARS' RULE:

An expert is anyone from out of town.

## WEBER'S DEFINITION:

An expert is one who knows more and more about less and less until he or she knows absolutely everything about nothing.

## MacDONALD'S LAW:

Consultants are mystical people who ask a company for a number and then give it back to them.

## WARREN'S RULE:

To spot the expert, pick the one who predicts the job will take the longest and cost the most.

## WINGER'S RULE:

If it sits on your desk for fifteen minutes, you've just become the expert.

## SCHROEDER'S LAW:

Indecision is the basis for flexibility.

## FAGIN'S RULE ON PAST PREDICTION:

Hindsight is an exact science.

## GREEN'S LAW OF DEBATE:

Anything is possible if you don't know what you're talking about.

## BURKE'S RULE:

Never create a problem for which you do not have the answer.

## Corollary:

Create problems for which only you have the answer.

## MATZ'S MAXIM:

A conclusion is the place where you got tired of thinking.

## LEVY'S FIRST LAW:

No amount of genius can overcome a preoccupation with detail.

## LEVY'S SECOND LAW:

Only God can make a random selection.

## BUCY'S LAW:

Nothing is ever accomplished by a reasonable man.

## DUNLAP'S LAWS OF PHYSICS:
1. Fact is solidified opinion.
2. Facts may weaken under extreme heat and pressure.
3. Truth is elastic.

## MERKIN'S MAXIM:
When in doubt, predict that the trend will continue.

## HALGREN'S SOLUTION:
When in trouble, obfuscate.

## HAWKINS' THEORY OF PROGRESS:
Progress does not consist in replacing a theory that is wrong with one that is right. It consists in replacing a theory that is wrong with one that is more subtly wrong.

## MEYER'S LAW:
It is a simple task to make things complex, but a complex task to make them simple.

## HLADE'S LAW:
If you have a difficult task, give it to a lazy man — he will find an easier way to do it.

# ACCOUNTSMANSHIP

## FROTHINGHAM'S FALLACY:

Time is money.

## CRANE'S LAW:

There ain't no such thing as a free lunch.

## TUCCILLE'S LAW OF REALITY:

Industry always moves in to fill an economic vacuum.

## WESTHEIMER'S RULE:

To estimate the time it takes to do a task: estimate the time you think it should take, multiply by two and change the unit of measure to the next highest unit. Thus we allocate two days for a one-hour task.

## EDWARDS' TIME/EFFORT LAW:

Effort x Time = Constant

1. Given a large initial time to do something, the initial effort will be small.
2. As time goes to zero, effort goes to infinity.

   **Corollary:** If it weren't for the last minute, nothing would get done.

## GRESHAM'S LAW:

Trivial matters are handled promptly; important matters are never solved.

## GRAY'S LAW OF PROGRAMMING:

"N+1" trivial tasks are expected to be accomplished in the same time as "n" tasks.

## LOGG'S REBUTTAL TO GRAY'S LAW:

"N+1" trivial tasks take twice as long as "n" trivial tasks.

## THE 90/90 RULE
## OF PROJECT SCHEDULES:

The first 90 percent of the task takes 90 percent of the time, and the last 10 percent takes the other 90 percent.

## WEINBERG'S LAW:

Progress is made on alternate Fridays.

## THE ORDERING PRINCIPLE:

Those supplies necessary for yesterday's experiment must be ordered no later than tomorrow noon.

## CHEOPS' LAW:

Nothing ever gets built on schedule or within budget.

## EXTENDED EPSTEIN-HEISENBERG PRINCIPLE:

In an R & D orbit, only two of the existing three parameters can be defined simultaneously. The parameters are task, time and resources.

1. If one knows what the task is, and there is a time limit allowed for the completion of the task, then one cannot guess how much it will cost.
2. If the time and resources are clearly defined, then it is impossible to know what part of the R & D task will be performed.
3. If you are given a clearly defined R & D goal and a definite amount of money that has been calculated to be necessary for the completion of the task, you cannot predict if and when the goal will be reached.

If one is lucky enough and can accurately define all three parameters, then what one deals with is not in the realm of R & D.

## PARETO'S LAW (THE 20/80 LAW):

Twenty percent of the customers account for 80 percent of the turnover.

Twenty percent of the components account for 80 percent of the cost.

## O'BRIEN'S PRINCIPLE
## (THE $357.73 THEORY):

Auditors always reject any expense account with a bottom line divisible by five or ten.

## ISSAWI'S OBSERVATION
## ON THE CONSUMPTION OF PAPER:

Each system has its own way of consuming vast amounts of paper: socialist societies fill out large forms in quadruplicate; capitalist societies put up huge posters and wrap every article in four layers of cardboard.

## BROWN'S LAW OF BUSINESS SUCCESS:

Our customer's paperwork is profit. Our own paperwork is loss.

## JOHN'S COLLATERAL COROLLARY:
In order to get a loan you must first prove you don't need it.

## BRIEN'S LAW:
At some time in the life cycle of virtually every organization, its ability to succeed in spite of itself runs out.

## LAW OF INSTITUTIONS:
The opulence of the front-office decor varies inversely with the fundamental solvency of the firm.

## PAULG'S LAW:
In America, it's not how much an item costs, it's how much you save.

## PERLSWEIG'S FIRST LAW:
People who can least afford to pay rent, pay rent. People who can most afford to pay rent, build up equity.

## JUHANI'S LAW:
The compromise will always be more expensive than either of the suggestions it is compromising.

# DESIGNSMANSHIP

## POULSEN'S PROPHECY:

If anything is used to its full potential, it will break.

## MAYNE'S LAW:

Nobody notices the big errors.

## PRINCIPLE OF DESIGN INERTIA:

Any change looks terrible at first.

## ENG'S PRINCIPLE:

The easier it is to do, the harder it is to change.

## WALLACE WOOD'S RULE OF DRAWING:

1. Never draw what you can copy.
2. Never copy what you can trace.
3. Never trace what you can cut out and paste down.

## ROBERTSON'S LAW:

Quality assurance doesn't.

## WRIGHT'S LAW OF QUALITY:

Quality is inversely proportional to the time left for completion of the project.

## LAW OF CORPORATE PLANNING:

Anything that can be changed will be changed until there is no time left to change anything.

## GORE'S LAWS OF DESIGN ENGINEERING:

1. The primary function of the design engineer is to make things difficult for the fabricator and impossible for the serviceman.
2. That component of any circuit which has the shortest service life will be placed in the least accessible location.
3. Any circuit design must contain at least one part that is obsolete, two parts that are unobtainable and three parts that are still under development.

### Corollaries:

A. The project engineer will change the design to suit the state of the art.

B. The changes will not be mentioned in the service manual.

## THE BASIC LAW OF CONSTRUCTION:

Cut it large and kick it into place.

## MEISSNER'S LAW:

Any producing entity is the last to use its own product.

## FIRST LAW FOR FREE-LANCE ARTISTS:

A high-paying rush job comes in only after you have committed to a low-paying rush job.

## SECOND LAW FOR FREE-LANCE ARTISTS:

All rush jobs are due the same day.

## THIRD LAW FOR FREE-LANCE ARTISTS:

The rush job you spent all night on won't be needed for at least two days.

## MacPHERSON'S THEORY OF ENTROPY:

It requires less energy to take an object out of its proper place than to put it back.

## SCHRANK'S FIRST LAW:

If it doesn't work, expand it.

### Corollary:

The greater the magnitude, the less notice will be taken that it does not work.

## BITTON'S POSTULATE ON STATE-OF-THE-ART ELECTRONICS:

If you understand it, it's obsolete.

## JOSE'S AXIOM:

Nothing is as temporary as that which is called permanent.

### Corollary:

Nothing is as permanent as that which is called temporary.

## OSBORN'S LAW:

Variables won't; constants aren't.

## KLIPSTEIN'S LAW OF SPECIFICATION:

In specifications, Murphy's Law supersedes Ohm's.

## FIRST LAW OF REVISION:

Information necessitating a change of design will be conveyed to the designer after — and only after — the plans are complete. (Often called the "Now They Tell Us!" Law.)

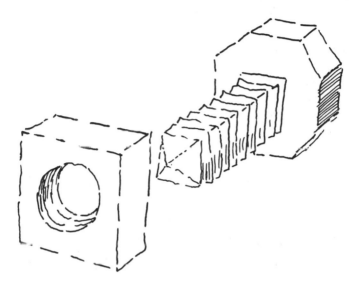

## Corollary:

In simple cases, presenting one obvious right way versus one obvious wrong way, it is often wiser to choose the wrong way, so as to expedite subsequent revision.

## SECOND LAW OF REVISION:

The more innocuous the modification appears to be, the further its influence will extend and the more plans will have to be redrawn.

## THIRD LAW OF REVISION:

If, when completion of a design is imminent, field dimensions are finally supplied as they actually are — instead of as they were meant to be — it is always simpler to start all over.

## Corollary:

It is usually impractical to worry beforehand about interferences — if you have none, someone will make one for you.

## LAW OF THE LOST INCH:

In designing any type of construction, no overall dimension can be totalled correctly after 4:40 P.M. on Friday.

## Corollaries:

1. Under the same conditions, if any minor dimensions are given to sixteenths of an inch, they cannot be totalled at all.
2. The correct total will become self-evident at 9:01 A.M. on Monday.

## LAWS OF APPLIED CONFUSION:

1. The one piece that the plant forgot to ship is the one that supports 75 percent of the balance of the shipment.

**Corollary:** Not only did the plant forget to ship it, 50 percent of the time they haven't even made it.

2. Truck deliveries that normally take one day will take five when you are waiting for the truck.

3. After adding two weeks to the schedule for unexpected delays, add two more for the unexpected, unexpected delays.

4. In any structure, pick out the one piece that should not be mismarked and expect the plant to cross you up.

**Corollaries:**

a. In any group of pieces with the same erection mark on it, one should not have that mark on it.

b. It will not be discovered until you try to put it where the mark says it's supposed to go.

c. Never argue with the fabricating plant about an error. The inspection prints are all checked off, even to the holes that aren't there.

## WYSZKOWSKI'S THEOREM:

Regardless of the units used by either the supplier or the customer, the manufacturer shall use his or her own arbitrary units convertible to those of either the supplier or the customer only by means of weird and unnatural conversion factors.

## THE SNAFU EQUATIONS:

1. Given any problem containing "n" equations, there will always be "n+1" unknowns.
2. An object or bit of information most needed will be the least available.
3. Once you have exhausted all possibilities and fail, there will be one solution, simple and obvious, highly visible to everyone else.
4. Badness comes in waves.

## SKINNER'S CONSTANT (FLANNAGAN'S FINAGLING FACTOR):

That quantity which, when multiplied by, divided by, added to, or subtracted from the answer you get, gives you the answer you should have gotten.

## SHAW'S PRINCIPLE:

Build a system that even a fool can use, and only a fool will want to use it.

## LAST LAW OF PRODUCT DESIGN:
If you can't fix it, feature it.

# MACHINESMANSHIP

## IBM POLLYANNA PRINCIPLE:

Machines should work; people should think.

## WASHLESKY'S LAW:

Anything is easier to take apart than to put together.

## RUDNICKI'S RULE:

That which cannot be taken apart will fall apart.

## RAP'S LAW OF INANIMATE REPRODUCTION:

If you take something apart and put it back together enough times, eventually you will have two of them.

## BEACH'S LAW:

No two identical parts are alike.

## WILLOUGHBY'S LAW:

When you try to prove to someone that a machine won't work, it will.

## ANTHONY'S LAW OF THE WORKSHOP:

Any tool, when dropped, will roll into the least accessible corner of the workshop.

## Corollary:

On the way to the corner, any dropped tool will first strike your toes.

# THE SPARE PARTS PRINCIPLE:

The accessibility, during recovery of small parts that fall from the workbench, varies directly with the size of the part — and inversely with its importance to the completion of work underway.

# SPECIAL LAW:

The workbench is always untidier than last time.

# GENERAL LAW:

The chaos in the universe always increases.

# FOUR WORKSHOP PRINCIPLES:

1. The one wrench or drill bit you need will be the one missing from the tool chest.
2. Most projects require three hands.
3. Leftover nuts never match leftover bolts.
4. The more carefully you plan a project, the more confusion there is when something goes wrong.

## RAY'S RULE FOR PRECISION:

Measure with a micrometer.
Mark with chalk.
Cut with an axe.

## LAW OF REPAIR:

You can't fix it if it ain't broke.

## RULE OF INTELLIGENT TINKERING:

Save all the parts.

## JOHNSON'S LAW:

When any mechanical contrivance fails, it will do
so at the most inconvenient possible time.

## LAWS OF ANNOYANCE:

When working on a project, if you put away a tool
that you're certain you're finished with, you will
need it instantly.

## WATSON'S LAW:

The reliability of machinery is inversely
proportional to the number and significance of
any persons watching it.

## WYSZKOWSKI'S LAW:

Anything can be made to work if you fiddle with it long enough.

## SATTINGER'S LAW:

It works better if you plug it in.

## LOWERY'S LAW:

If it jams — force it. If it breaks, it needed replacing anyway.

## THE VCR RULE:

The most expensive special feature on the VCR never gets used.

## SCHMIDT'S LAW:

If you mess with a thing long enough, it'll break.

## FUDD'S LAW OF OPPOSITION:

Push something hard enough, and it will fall over.

## ANTHONY'S LAW OF FORCE:

Don't force it; get a larger hammer.

## HORNER'S FIVE-THUMB POSTULATE:

Experience varies directly with equipment ruined.

## CAHN'S AXIOM:
When all else fails, read the instructions.

## THE PRINCIPLE CONCERNING MULTIFUNCTIONAL DEVICES:
The fewer functions any device is required to perform, the more perfectly it can perform those functions.

## JENKINSON'S LAW:
It won't work.

# RESEARCHMANSHIP

## GORDON'S LAW:

If a research project is not worth doing at all, it is not worth doing well.

## MURPHY'S LAW OF RESEARCH:

Enough research will tend to support your theory.

## MAIER'S LAW:

If the facts do not conform to the theory, they must be disposed of.

### Corollaries:

1. The bigger the theory, the better.
2. The experiment may be considered a success if no more than 50 percent of the observed measurements must be discarded to obtain a correspondence with the theory.

## WILLIAMS AND HOLLAND'S LAW:

If enough data are collected, anything may be proven by statistical methods.

## EDINGTON'S THEORY:

The number of different hypotheses erected to explain a given biological phenomenon is inversely proportional to the available knowledge.

# HARVARD'S LAW:

Under the most rigorously controlled conditions of pressure, temperature, volume, humidity and other variables, the organism will do as it damn well pleases.

# FOURTH LAW OF REVISION:

After painstaking and careful analysis of a sample, you are always told that it is the wrong sample and doesn't apply to the problem.

# HERSH'S LAW:

Biochemistry expands to fill the space and time available for its completion and publication.

# FINAGLE'S FIRST LAW:

If an experiment works, something has gone wrong.

# FINAGLE'S SECOND LAW:

No matter what the anticipated result, there will always be someone eager to (a) misinterpret it, (b) fake it, or (c) believe it happened to their own pet theory.

# FINAGLE'S THIRD LAW:

In any collection of data, the figure most obviously correct, beyond all need of checking, is the mistake.

## Corollaries:

1. No one whom you ask for help will see it.
2. Everyone who stops by with unsought advice will see it immediately.

## FINAGLE'S FOURTH LAW:

Once a job is fouled up, anything done to improve it only makes it worse.

## FINAGLE'S RULES:

1. To study a subject best, understand it thoroughly before you start.
2. Always keep a record of data — it indicates you've been working.
3. Always draw your curves, then plot your reading.
4. In case of doubt, make it sound convincing.
5. Experiments should be reproducible — they should all fail in the same way.
6. Do not believe in miracles — rely on them.

## WINGO'S AXIOM:

All Finagle Laws may be bypassed by learning the simple art of doing without thinking.

## RULE OF ACCURACY:

When working toward the solution of a problem, it always helps if you know the answer.

## YOUNG'S LAW:

All great discoveries are made by mistake.

## Corollary:

The greater the funding, the longer it takes to make the mistake.

## FETT'S LAW OF THE LAB:

Never replicate a successful experiment.

## WYSZOWSKI'S LAW:

No experiment is reproducible.

## FUTILITY FACTOR:

No experiment is ever a complete failure — it can always serve as a negative example.

## PARKINSON'S LAW OF SCIENTIFIC PROGRESS:

The progress of science varies inversely with the number of journals published.

## WHOLE PICTURE PRINCIPLE:

Research scientists are so wrapped up in their own narrow endeavors that they cannot possibly see the whole picture of anything, including their own research.

## Corollary:

The Director of Research should know as little as possible about the specific subject of research he or she is administering.

## BROOKE'S LAW:

Whenever a system becomes completely defined, some damn fool discovers something that either abolishes the system or expands it beyond recognition.

## CAMPBELL'S LAW:

Nature abhors a vacuous experimenter.

## FREIVALD'S LAW:

Only a fool can reproduce another fool's work.

## TENENBAUM'S LAW OF REPLICABILITY:

The most interesting results happen only once.

## SOUDER'S LAW:

Repetition does not establish validity.

## HANGGI'S LAW:

The more trivial your research, the more people will read it and agree.

## Corollary:

The more vital your research, the less people will understand it.

## HANDY GUIDE TO MODERN SCIENCE:

1. If it's green or it wriggles, it's biology.
2. If it stinks, it's chemistry.
3. If it doesn't work, it's physics.

## CERF'S EXTENSIONS TO THE HANDY GUIDE TO MODERN SCIENCE:

4. If it's incomprehensible, it's mathematics.
5. If it doesn't make sense, it's either economics or psychology.

## YOUNG'S COMMENT ON SCIENTIFIC METHOD:

You can't get here from there.

## MACBETH'S COMMENT ON EVOLUTION:

The best theory is not *ipso facto* a good theory.

## BARR'S INERTIAL PRINCIPLE:

Asking scientists to revise their theory is like asking cops to revise the law.

## THE SAGAN FALLACY:

To say a human being is nothing but molecules is like saying a Shakespearean play is nothing but words.

## EINSTEIN'S OBSERVATION:

Inasmuch as the mathematical theorems are related to reality, they are not sure; inasmuch as they are sure, they are not related to reality.

## THE RELIABILITY PRINCIPLE:

The difference between the Laws of Nature and Murphy's Law is that with the Laws of Nature you can count on things screwing up the same way every time.

## DARWIN'S LAW:

Nature will tell you a direct lie if she can.

## BLOCH'S EXTENSION:

So will Darwinists.

## FIRST LAW OF SCIENTIFIC PROGRESS:

The advance of science can be measured by the rate at which exceptions to previously held laws accumulate.

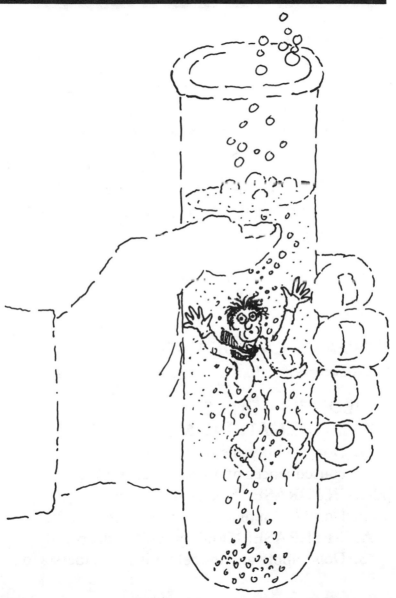

## Corollaries:

1. Exceptions always outnumber rules.
2. There are always exceptions to established exceptions.
3. By the time one masters the exceptions, no one recalls the rules to which they apply.

## FIRST LAW OF PARTICLE PHYSICS:

The shorter the life of the particle, the more it costs to produce.

## SECOND LAW OF PARTICLE PHYSICS:

The basic building blocks of matter do not occur in nature.

## FINMAN'S LAW OF MATHEMATICS:

Nobody wants to read anyone else's formulas.

## GOLOMB'S DON'TS OF MATHEMATICAL MODELING:

1. Don't believe the thirty-third-order consequences of a first-order model.

CATCH PHRASE: *"Cum grano salis."*

2. Don't extrapolate beyond the region of fit.

CATCH PHRASE: "Don't go off the deep end."

3. Don't apply any model until you understand

the simplifying assumptions on which it is based, and can test their applicability.

CATCH PHRASE: "Use only as directed."

4. Don't believe that the model is the reality.

CATCH PHRASE: "Don't eat the menu."

5. Don't distort reality to fit the model.

CATCH PHRASE: "The 'Procrustes Method.' "

6. Don't limit yourself to a single model: more than one may be useful for understanding diffcrent aspects of the same phenomenon.

CATCH PHRASE: "Legalize polygamy."

7. Don't retain a discredited model.

CATCH PHRASE: "Don't beat a dead horse."

8. Don't fall in love with your model.

CATCH PHRASE: "Pygmalion."

9. Don't apply the terminology of Subject A to the problems of Subject B if it is to the enrichment of neither.

CATCH PHRASE: "New names for old."

10. Don't expect that by having named a demon you have destroyed him.

CATCH PHRASE: "Rumpelstiltskin."

## LAW OF LABORATORY WORK:

Hot glass looks exactly the same as cold glass.

## FELSON'S LAW:

To steal ideas from one person is plagiarism; to steal from many is research.

## VALERY'S LAW:

History is the science of what never happens twice.

## DARROW'S COMMENT ON HISTORY:

History repeats itself. That's one of the things wrong with history.

## PRIMARY RULE OF HISTORY:

History doesn't repeat itself—historians merely repeat each other.

## PAVLU'S RULES FOR ECONOMY IN RESEARCH:

1. Deny the last established truth on the list.
2. Add yours.
3. Pass the list.

## MR. COOPER'S LAW:

If you do not understand a particular word in a piece of technical writing, ignore it. The piece will make perfect sense without it.

## BOGOVICH'S COROLLARY TO MR. COOPER'S LAW:

If the piece makes no sense without the word, it will make no sense with the word.

## GROUND RULE FOR LABORATORY WORKERS:

When you do not know what you are doing, do it neatly.

## FINAGLE'S RULE:

Teamwork is essential. It allows you to blame someone else.

## FINAGLE'S CREED:

Science is true. Don't be misled by facts.

## MUENCH'S LAW:

Nothing improves an innovation like lack of controls.

## MAY'S LAW OF STRATIGRAPHY:

The quality of correlation is inversely proportional to the density of control.

## VESILIND'S LAW OF EXPERIMENTATION:

1. If reproducibility may be a problem, conduct the test only once.
2. If a straight line fit is required, obtain only two data points.

## LERMAN'S LAW OF TECHNOLOGY:

Any technical problem can be overcome given enough time and money.

### Lerman's Corollary:

You are never given enough time or money.

## ROCKY'S LEMMA OF INNOVATION PREVENTION:

Unless the results are known in advance, funding agencies will reject the proposal.

## THUMB'S FIRST POSTULATE:

It is better to solve a problem with a crude approximation and know the truth, plus or minus 10 percent, than to demand an exact solution and not know the truth at all.

## THUMB'S SECOND POSTULATE:

An easily understood, workable falsehood is more useful than a complex, incomprehensible truth.

## JONES' LAW:

Anyone who makes a significant contribution to any field of endeavor, and stays in that field long enough, becomes an obstruction to its progress — in direct proportion to the importance of the original contribution.

## MANN'S LAW (generalized):

If a scientist uncovers a publishable fact, it will become central to his theory.

## Corollary:

His theory, in turn, will become central to all scientific thought.

## THE RULER RULE:

There is no such thing as a straight line.

## GRELB'S LAW OF ERRORING:

In any series of calculations, errors tend to occur at the opposite end from which you begin checking.

## ROBERT'S AXIOM:

Only errors exist.

## Berman's Corollary to Robert's Axiom:

One man's error is another man's data.

# COMPUTER MURPHOLOGY

## LAW OF UNRELIABILITY:

To err is human, but to really foul things up requires a computer.

## GREER'S LAW:

A computer program does what you tell it to do, not what you want it to do.

## SUTIN'S LAW:

The most useless computer tasks are the most fun to do.

## McCRISTY'S COMPUTER AXIOMS:

1. Back-up files are never complete.
2. Software bugs are correctable only after the software is judged obsolete by the industry.

## LEO BEISER'S COMPUTER AXIOM:

When putting it into memory, remember where you put it.

## STEINBACH'S GUIDELINE FOR SYSTEMS PROGRAMMING:

Never test for an error condition you don't know how to handle.

## MANUBAY'S LAWS FOR PROGRAMMERS:

1. If a programmer's modification of an existing program works, it's probably not what the users want.
2. Users don't know what they really want, but they know for certain what they don't want.

## LAWS OF COMPUTER PROGRAMMING:

1. Any given program, when running, is obsolete.
2. Any given program costs more and takes longer.
3. If a program is useful, it will have to be changed.
4. If a program is useless, it will have to be documented.
5. Any given program will expand to fill all available memory.
6. The value of a program is proportional to the weight of its output.
7. Program complexity grows until it exceeds the capability of the programmer who must maintain it.

# TROUTMAN'S PROGRAMMING POSTULATES:

1. If a test installation functions perfectly, all subsequent systems will malfunction.
2. Not until a program has been in production for at least six months will the most harmful error be discovered.
3. Job control cards that positively cannot be arranged in improper order will be.
4. Interchangeable tapes won't.
5. If the input editor has been designed to reject all bad input, an ingenious idiot will discover a method to get bad data past him or her.
6. Profanity is the one language all programmers know best.

# GILB'S LAWS OF UNRELIABILITY:

1. Computers are unreliable, but humans are even more unreliable.
2. Any system that depends on human reliability is unreliable.
3. Undetectable errors are infinite in variety, in contrast to detectable errors, which by definition are limited.

4. Investment in reliability will increase until it exceeds the probable cost of errors, or until someone insists on getting some useful work done.

## BROOK'S LAW:

Adding manpower to a late software project makes it later.

## LAWS OF COMPUTERDOM ACCORDING TO GOLUB:

1. Fuzzy project objectives are used to avoid the embarrassment of estimating the corresponding costs.
2. A carelessly planned project takes three times longer to complete than expected; a carefully planned project takes only twice as long.
3. The effort required to correct a course increases geometrically with time.
4. Project teams detest weekly progress reporting because it so vividly displays their lack of progress.

## SMITH'S LAW OF COMPUTER REPAIR:

Access holes will be half an inch too small.

## Corollary:

Holes that are the right size will be in the wrong place.

## JARUK'S LAW:

If it would be cheaper to buy a new unit, the company will insist upon repairing the old one.

## Corollary:

If it would be cheaper to repair the old one, the company will insist on the latest model.

## WEINBERG'S FIRST LAW:

If builders built buildings the way programmers wrote programs, then the first woodpecker that came along would destroy civilization.

## LUBARSKY'S LAW OF CYBERNETIC ENTOMOLOGY:

There's always one more bug.

# ACADEMIOLOGY

## H.L. MENCKEN'S LAW:

Those who can, do.

Those who cannot, teach.

## Martin's Extension:

Those who cannot teach, administrate.

## ELLARD'S LAW:

Those who want to learn will learn.

Those who do not want to learn will lead enterprises.

Those incapable of either learning or leading will regulate scholarship and enterprise to death.

## MEREDITH'S LAW FOR GRAD SCHOOL SURVIVAL:

Never let your major professor know that you exist.

## VILE'S LAW FOR EDUCATORS:

No one is listening until you make a mistake.

## VILE'S LAW OF GRADING PAPERS:

All papers after the top are upside down or backwards, until you right the pile. Then the process repeats.

# WEINER'S LAW OF LIBRARIES:

There are no answers, only cross-references.

# LAWS OF CLASS SCHEDULING:

1. If the course you wanted most has room for "n" students, you will be the "n+1" to apply.

2. Class schedules are designed so that every student will waste maximum time between classes.

   **Corollary:** When you are occasionally able to schedule two classes in a row, they will be held in classrooms at opposite ends of the campus.

3. A prerequisite for a desired course will be offered only during the semester following the desired course.

# LAWS OF APPLIED TERROR:

1. When reviewing your notes before an exam, the most important ones will be illegible.

2. The more studying you did for the exam, the less sure you are as to which answer they want.

3. Eighty percent of the final exam will be based on the one lecture you missed about the one book you didn't read.

4. The night before the English history midterm, your Biology instructor will assign two hundred pages on planaria.

## Corollary:

Every instructor assumes that you have nothing else to do except study for that instructor's course.

5. If you are given an open-book exam, you will forget your book.

    **Corollary:** If you are given a take-home exam, you will forget where you live.

6. At the end of the semester you will recall having enrolled in a course at the beginning of the semester — and never attending.

## FIRST LAW OF FINAL EXAMS:

Pocket calculator batteries that have lasted all semester will fail during the math final.

## Corollary:

If you bring extra batteries, they will be defective.

## SECOND LAW OF FINAL EXAMS:

In your toughest final, the most distractingly attractive student in class will sit next to you for the first time.

## SEEGER'S LAW:

Anything in parentheses can be ignored.

## NATALIE'S LAW OF ALGEBRA:

You never catch on until after the test.

## SEIT'S LAW OF HIGHER EDUCATION:

The one course you must take to graduate will not be offered during your last semester.

## MURPHY'S RULE OF THE TERM PAPER:

The book or periodical most vital to the completion of your term paper will be missing from the library.

## Corollary:

If it is available, the most important page will be torn out.

## DUGGAN'S LAW OF SCHOLARLY RESEARCH:

The most valuable quotation will be the one for which you cannot determine the source.

## Corollary:

The source for an unattributed quotation will appear in the most hostile review of your work.

## ROMINGER'S RULES FOR STUDENTS:

1. The more general the title of a course, the less you will learn from it.
2. The more specific a title is, the less you will be able to apply it later.

## HANSEN'S LIBRARY AXIOM:

The closest library doesn't have the material you need.

## LONDON'S LAW OF LIBRARIES:

No matter which book you need, it's on the bottom shelf.

## ATWOOD'S COROLLARY:

No books are lost by lending except those you particularly want to keep.

## JOHNSON'S LAW:

If you miss one issue of any magazine, it will be the issue that contained the article, story or installment you were most anxious to read.

### Corollary:

All of your friends either missed it, lost it or threw it out.

# WHITTINGTON'S LAW OF COMMUNICATION:

When a writer prepares a manuscript on a subject he or she does not understand, the work will be understood only by readers who know more about that subject than the writer does.

## Corollary:

Writings prepared without understanding must fail in the first objective of communication — informing the uninformed.

## KERR-MARTIN LAW:

1. In dealing with their *own* problems, faculty members are the most extreme conservatives.
2. In dealing with *other* people's problems, they are the most extreme liberals.

# ROMINGER'S RULES FOR TEACHERS:

1. When a student asks for a second time if you have read his book report, he did not read the book.
2. If attendance is mandatory, a scheduled exam will produce increased absenteeism. If attendance is optional, an exam will produce persons you have never seen before.

# WORK AND OFFICE MURPHOLOGY

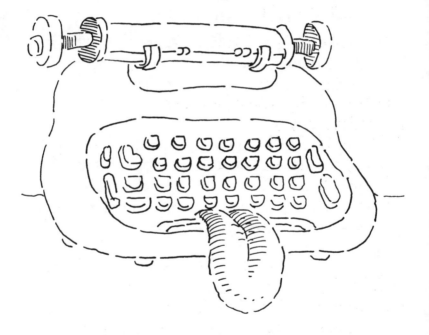

## HARDIN'S LAW:

You can never do just one thing.

## HECHT'S LAW:

There no time like the present for postponing what you don't want to do.

## GROSSMAN'S LEMMA:

Any task worth doing was worth doing yesterday.

## KNAGG'S DERIVATIVE OF MURPHY'S LAW:

The more complicated and grandiose the plan, the greater the chance of failure.

## DEHAY'S AXIOM:

Simple jobs always get put off because there will be time to do them later.

## WETHERN'S LAW OF SUSPENDED JUDGMENT:

Assumption is the mother of all screw-ups.

## KRANSKE'S LAW:

Beware of a day in which you don't have something to bitch about.

## PARKINSON'S FIRST LAW:

Work expands to fill the time available for its completion; the thing to be done swells in perceived importance and complexity in a direct ratio with the time to be spent in its completion.

## PARKINSON'S SECOND LAW:

Expenditures rise to meet income.

## PARKINSON'S THIRD LAW:

Expansion means complexity and complexity decays.

## PARKINSON'S FOURTH LAW:

The number of people in any working group tends to increase regardless of the amount of work to be done.

## THE EINSTEIN EXTENSION OF PARKINSON'S LAW:

A work project expands to fill the space available.

### Corollary:

No matter how large the work space, if two projects must be done at the same time they will require the use of the same part of the work space.

## SIX LAWS OF OFFICE MURPHOLOGY:

1. Important letters that contain no errors will develop errors in the mail.

   **Corollary:** Corresponding errors will show up in duplicate while the boss is reading it.

2. Office machines that function perfectly during normal business hours will break down when you return to the office at night to use them for personal business.

3. Machines that have broken down will work perfectly when the person who repairs them arrives.

4. Envelopes and stamps that don't stick when you lick them will stick to other things when you don't want them to.

5. Vital papers will demonstrate their vitality by moving from where you left them to where you can't find them.

6. The last person who quit or was fired will be held responsible for everything that goes wrong — until the next person quits or is fired.

## BOGOVICH'S LAW:

He who hesitates is probably right.

## DEVRIES' DILEMMA:

If you hit two keys on the typewriter, the one you don't want hits the paper.

## THEORY OF SELECTIVE SUPERVISION:

The one time in the day that you lean back and relax is the one time the boss walks through the office.

## LAUNEGAYER'S OBSERVATION:

Asking dumb questions is easier than correcting dumb mistakes.

## STRANO'S LAW:

When all else fails, try the boss's suggestion.

## BRINTNALL'S LAW:

If you are given two contradictory orders, obey them both.

## SHAPIRO'S LAW OF REWARD:

The one who does the least work will get the most credit.

## LAWS OF PROCRASTINATION:

1. Procrastination shortens the job and places the responsibility for its termination on someone else (the authority who imposed the deadline).

2. It reduces anxiety by reducing the expected quality of the project from the best of all possible efforts to the best that can be expected given the limited time.

3. Status is gained in the eyes of others, and in one's own eyes, because it is assumed that the importance of the work justifies the stress.

4. Avoidance of interruptions, including the assignment of other duties, can usually be achieved, so that the obviously stressed worker can concentrate on the single effort.

5. Procrastination avoids boredom; one never has the feeling that there is nothing important to do.

6. It may eliminate the job if the need to procrastinate passes before the job can be done.

## QUILE'S CONSULTATION LAW:

The job that pays the most will be offered when there is no time to deliver the services.

## DOANE'S LAWS OF PROCRASTINATION:

1. The more proficient one is at procrastination, the less proficient one need be at all else.
2. The slower one works, the fewer mistakes one makes.

## DREW'S LAW OF PROFESSIONAL PRACTICE:

The client who pays the least complains the most.

## JOHNSON'S LAW:

The number of minor illnesses among the employees is inversely proportional to the health of the organization.

## TILLIS' ORGANIZATIONAL PRINCIPLE:

If you file it, you'll know where it is but never need it.

If you don't file it, you'll need it but never know where it is.

## OWEN'S LAW FOR SECRETARIES:

As soon as you sit down to a cup of hot coffee, your boss will ask you to do something that will last until the coffee is cold.

## SANDILAND'S LAW:

Free time that unexpectedly becomes available will be wasted.

## SCOTT'S LAW OF BUSINESS:

Never walk down a hallway in an office building without a piece of paper in your hand.

## HARBOUR'S LAW:

The deadline is one week after the original deadline.

## EDDIE'S LAW OF BUSINESS:

Never conduct negotiations before 10:00 A.M. or after 4:00 P.M. Before ten you appear too anxious, and after four they think you're desperate.

## TABLE OF HANDY OFFICE EXCUSES:

1. That's the way we've always done it.
2. I didn't know you were in a hurry for it.
3. No one told me to go ahead.
4. I'm waiting for an OK.
5. How did I know this was different?
6. That's his job, not mine.
7. Wait 'til the boss comes back and ask her.
8. We don't make many mistakes.
9. I didn't think it was very important.
10. I'm so busy, I just can't get around to it.
11. I thought I told you.
12. I wasn't hired to do that.

## DRUMMOND'S LAW OF PERSONNEL RECRUITING:

The ideal resume will turn up one day after the position is filled.

## FOX ON YESMANSHIP:

It's worth scheming to be the bearer of good news.

## Corollary:

Don't be in the building when bad news arrives.

## PINTO'S LAW:

Do someone a favor and it becomes your job.

## CONNOR'S LAW:

If something is confidential, it will be left in the copier machine.

## LANGSAM'S ORNITHOLOGICAL AXIOM:

It's difficult to soar with eagles when you work with turkeys.

# SYSTEMANTICS*

*(from *Systemantics* by John Gall; Quandrangle/New York Times Book Co., 1977)

# THE FUNDAMENTAL THEOREM:

New systems generate new problems.

## Corollary:

Systems should not be unnecessarily multiplied.

# THE GENERALIZED UNCERTAINTY PRINCIPLE:

Systems tend to grow, and as they grow, they encroach.

Alternative Formulations:

1. Complicated systems produce unexpected outcomes.
2. The total behavior of large systems cannot be predicted.

## Corollary: The Non-Additivity Theorem of Systems-Behavior

A large system, produced by expanding the dimensions of a smaller system, does not behave like the smaller system.

# THE FUNCTIONARY FALSITY:

People in systems do not do what the system says they are doing.

## THE OPERATIONAL FALLACY:

The system itself does not do what it says it is doing.

# FIRST LAW OF SYSTEMANTICS:

A complex system that works is invariably found to have evolved from a simple system that works.

# SECOND LAW OF SYSTEMANTICS:

A complex system designed from scratch never works and cannot be patched up to make it work. You have to start over, beginning with a working simple system.

# THE FUNDAMENTAL POSTULATES OF ADVANCED SYSTEMS THEORY:

1. Everything is a system.
2. Everything is part of a larger system.
3. The universe is infinitely systematized, both upward (larger systems) and downward (smaller systems).
4. All systems are infinitely complex. (The illusion of simplicity comes from focusing attention on one or a few variables.)

# LE CHATELIER'S PRINCIPLE:

Complex systems tend to oppose their own proper function.

# SITUATIONAL MURPHOLOGY

# DRAZEN'S LAW OF RESTITUTION:

The time it takes to rectify a situation is inversely proportional to the time it took to do the damage.

## Example:

It takes longer to glue a vase together than to break one.

## Example:

It takes longer to lose $x$ number of pounds than to gain $x$ number of pounds.

# ETORRE'S OBSERVATION:

The other line moves faster.

# O'BRIEN'S VARIATION ON ETORRE'S OBSERVATION:

If you change lines, the one you just left will start to move faster than the one you are now in.

## Kenton's Corollary:

Switching back screws up both lines and makes everybody angry.

# THE QUEUE PRINCIPLE:

The longer you wait in line, the greater the likelihood that you are standing in the wrong line.

## FLUGG'S RULE:

The slowest checker is always at the quick check-out lane.

## VILE'S LAW OF ADVANCED LINESMANSHIP:

1. If you're running for a short line, it suddenly becomes a long line.
2. When you're waiting in a long line, the people behind you are shunted to a new, short line.
3. If you step out of a short line for a second, it becomes a long line.
4. If you're in a short line, the people in front let in their friends and relatives and make it a long line.
5. A short line outside a building becomes a long line inside.
6. If you stand in one place long enough, you make a line.

## HEID'S LAW OF LINES:

No matter how early you arrive, someone else is in line first.

## LUPOSCHAINSKY'S HURRY-UP-AND-WAIT PRINCIPLE:

If you're early, it'll be cancelled.

If you knock yourself out to be on time, you'll have to wait.

If you're late, you'll be too late.

## DEDERA'S LAW:

In a three-story building served by one elevator, nine times out of ten the elevator car will be on a floor where you are not.

## GLUCK'S LAW:

Whichever way you turn upon entering an elevator, the buttons will be on the opposite side.

## LYNCH'S LAW:

The elevator always comes after you have put down your bag.

## WITTEN'S LAW:

Whenever you cut your fingernails you will find a need for them an hour later.

## STORRY'S PRINCIPLE OF CRIMINAL INDICTMENT:

The degree of guilt is directly proportional to the intensity of the denial.

## TRACY'S TIME OBSERVATION:

Good times end too quickly. Bad times go on forever.

## THIESSEN'S LAW OF ART:

The overwhelming prerequisite for the greatness of an artist is that artist's death.

## ELY'S LAW:

Wear the right costume and the part plays itself.

## FIRST RULE OF ACTING:

Whatever happens, look as if it was intended.

## ZADRA'S LAW OF BIOMECHANICS:

The severity of the itch is inversely proportional to the reach.

## THIESSEN'S LAW OF GASTRONOMY:

The hardness of the butter is in direct proportion to the softness of the roll.

## REVEREND CHICHESTER'S LAWS:

1. If the weather is extremely bad, church attendance will be down.
2. If the weather is extremely good, church attendance will be down.
3. If the bulletins are in short supply, church attendance will exceed all expectations.

## LAW OF BALANCE:

Bad habits will cancel out good ones.
Example: The orange juice and granola you had for breakfast will be canceled out by the cigarett~ you smoked on the way to work and the candy bar you just bought.

## CAFETERIA LAW:

The item you had your eye on the minute you walked in will be taken by the person in front of you.

## DINER'S DILEMMA:

A clean tie attracts the soup of the day.

## REYNOLD'S LAW OF CLIMATOLOGY:

Wind velocity increases directly with the cost of the hairdo.

## JAN AND MARTHA'S LAW OF THE BEAUTY SHOP:

The most flattering comments on your hair come the day before you're scheduled to have it cut.

## JILLY'S LAW:

The worse the haircut, the slower it grows out.

## HUTCHINSON'S LAW:

If a situation requires undivided attention, it will occur simultaneously with a compelling distraction.

## FULLER'S LAW OF JOURNALISM:

The farther away the disaster or accident occurs, the greater the number of dead and injured required for it to become a story.

## LAWS OF TRUTH IN REPORTING:

1. The closer you are to the facts of a situation, the more obvious are the errors in the news coverage.
2. The farther you are from the facts of a situation, the more you tend to believe the news coverage.

## WEATHERWAX'S POSTULATE:

The degree to which you overreact to information will be in inverse proportion to its accuracy.

## DAVIS' LAW:

If a headline ends in a question mark, the answer is "no."

## WEAVER'S LAW:

When several reporters share a cab on an assignment, the reporter in the front seat pays for all.

## Doyle's Corollary:

No matter how many reporters share a cab, and no matter who pays, each puts the full fare on his or her own expense account.

## THE LAW OF THE LETTER:

The best way to inspire fresh thoughts is to seal the letter.

## HOWDEN'S LAW:

You remember to mail a letter only when you're nowhere near a mailbox.

## LAWS OF POSTAL DELIVERY:

1. Love letters, business contracts and money you are due always arrive three weeks late.
2. Junk mail arrives the day it was sent.

## JONES' LAW OF ZOOS AND MUSEUMS:

The most interesting specimen will not be labeled.

## LAW OF CHRISTMAS DECORATING:

The outdoor lights that tested perfectly develop burn-outs as soon as they are strung on the house.

## MILSTEAD'S CHRISTMAS CARD RULE:

After you have mailed your last card, you will receive a card from someone you overlooked.

## JONES' LAW OF PUBLISHING:

Some errors will always go unnoticed until the book is in print.

### Bloch's Corollary:

The first page the author turns to upon receiving an advance copy will be the page containing the worst error.

# PHOTOGRAPHER'S LAWS:

1. The best shots happen immediately after the last frame is exposed.
2. The other best shots are generally attempted through the lens cap.
3. Any surviving best shots are ruined when someone inadvertently opens the darkroom door and all of the dark leaks out.

# DOWLING'S LAW OF PHOTOGRAPHY:

One missed photographic opportunity creates a desire to purchase two additional pieces of equipment.

# SIR WALTER'S LAW:

The tendency of smoke from a cigarette, barbecue or campfire to drift into a person's face varies directly with that person's sensitivity to smoke.

# KAUFFMAN'S LAW OF AIRPORTS:

The distance to the gate is inversely proportional to the time available to catch your flight.

# ROGERS' LAW:

As soon as the coffee is served, the airliner encounters turbulence.

## Davis' Explanation of Rogers' Law:

Serving coffee on an aircraft causes turbulence.

## BASIC BAGGAGE PRINCIPLE:

Whatever carousel you stand by, your baggage will come in on another one.

## ANGUS' EXCHANGE AXIOM:

When traveling overseas, the exchange rate improves markedly the day after one has purchased foreign currency.

## Corollary:

Upon returning home, the rate drops again as soon as one has converted all unused foreign currency.

## CROSBY'S LAW:

You can tell how bad a musical is by how many times the chorus yells, "Hooray!"

## BYRNE'S LAW OF CONCRETING:

When you pour, it rains.

## McLAUGHLIN'S LAW:

In a key position in every genealogy you will find a John Smith from London.

## WRIGHT'S LAW:

A doctor can bury his or her mistakes, but an architect can only advise the client to plant vines.

## RUSH'S RULE OF GRAVITY:

When you drop change at a vending machine, the pennies will fall nearby while the other coins will roll out of sight.

# SOCIOMURPHOLOGY
# (HUMANSHIP)

## SHIRLEY'S LAW:

Most people deserve each other.

## HARRIS' LAMENT:

All the good ones are taken.

## ARTHUR'S LAWS OF LOVE:

1. People to whom you are attracted invariably think you remind them of someone else.
2. The love letter you finally got the courage to send will be delayed in the mail long enough for you to make a fool of yourself in person.
3. Other people's romantic gestures seem novel and exciting. Your own romantic gestures seem foolish and clumsy.

## LAW OF HUMAN QUIRKS:

Everyone wants to be noticed, but no one wants to be stared at.

## ANDERSON'S AXIOM:

You can only be young once, but you can be immature forever.

## BEDFELLOW'S RULE:

The one who snores will fall asleep first.

## THOMS' LAW OF MARITAL BLISS:

The length of a marriage is inversely proportional to the amount spent on the wedding.

## MURPHY'S FIRST LAW FOR HUSBANDS:

The first time you go out after your wife's birthday you will see the gift you gave her marked down 50 percent.

### Corollary:

If she is with you, she will assume you chose it because it was cheap.

## MURPHY'S SECOND LAW FOR HUSBANDS:

The gifts you buy your wife are never as apropos as the gifts your neighbor buys his wife.

## MURPHY'S THIRD LAW FOR HUSBANDS:

Your wife's stored possessions will be on top of your stored possessions.

## MURPHY'S FIRST LAW FOR WIVES:

If you ask your husband to pick up five items at the supermarket and then add one more as an afterthought, he'll forget two of the first five.

## MURPHY'S SECOND LAW FOR WIVES:

The snapshots you take of your husband are always more flattering than the ones he takes of you.

## MURPHY'S THIRD LAW FOR WIVES:

Whatever arrangements you make for the division of household duties, your husband's job will be easier.

## GILLENSON'S (de-sexed) LAWS OF EXPECTATION:

1. Never get excited about a blind date because of how he or she sounds over the phone.
2. Never get excited about a person because of what he or she looks like from behind.

## COLVARD'S LOGICAL PREMISES:

All probabilities are 50 percent. Either a thing will happen or it won't.

### Colvard's Unconscionable Commentary:

This is especially true when dealing with women.

### Grelb's Commentary on Colvard's Premise:

Likelihoods, however, are 90 percent against you.

## CHEIT'S LAMENT:

If you help a friend in need, he is sure to remember you — the next time he is in need.

## FARMER'S CREDO:

Sow your wild oats on Saturday night — then on Sunday pray for crop failure.

## ESQUIRE'S COMMENT:

The better the relationship starts out, the faster it fades.

## RUBY'S PRINCIPLE OF CLOSE ENCOUNTERS:

The probability of meeting someone you know increases when you are with someone you don't want to be seen with.

## JOHNSON'S LAW:

If, in the course of several months, only three worthwhile social events take place, they will all fall on the same evening.

## DENNISTON'S LAW:

Virtue is its own punishment.

### Denniston's Corollary:

If you do something right once, someone will ask you to do it again.

### Bloch's Commentary:

Denniston's Corollary applies to the statement: "Virtuous action will never go unpunished." Denniston's Law has broader implications.

## MASON'S LAW OF SYNERGISM:

The one day you'd sell your soul for something, souls are a glut.

## RON'S OBSERVATIONS FOR TEENAGERS:

1. The pimples don't appear until the hour before the date.
2. The scratch on the record is always through the song you like most.

## JOHNSON AND LAIRD'S LAW:

A toothache tends to start on Saturday night.

## SCHRIMPTON'S LAW OF TEENAGE OPPORTUNITY:

When opportunity knocks, you've got headphones on.

## UNDERLYING PRINCIPLE OF SOCIO-GENETICS:

Superiority is recessive.

## PROFESSOR BLOCK'S MOTTO:

Forgive and remember.

## JACOB'S LAW:

To err is human — to blame it on someone else is even more human.

## EDELSTEIN'S ADVICE:

Don't worry over what other people are thinking about you. They're too busy worrying over what you are thinking about them.

## MEADER'S LAW:

Whatever happens to you, it will previously have happened to everyone you know.

## BOCKLAGE'S LAW:

He who laughs last—probably didn't get the joke.

## FIRST LAW OF SOCIO-GENETICS:

Celibacy is not hereditary.

## FARBER'S LAW:

Necessity is the mother of strange bedfellows.

## HARTLEY'S LAW:

Never sleep with anyone crazier than yourself.

## BECKHAP'S LAW:

Beauty times brains equals a constant.

## PARKER'S LAW:

Beauty is only skin deep, but ugly goes clean to the bone.

## PARDO'S POSTULATES:

1. Anything good in life is either illegal, immoral or fattening.
2. The three faithful things in life are money, a dog and an old woman.
3. Don't care if you're rich or not, as long as you can live comfortably and have everything you want.

## STEINKOPFF'S EXTENSION TO PARDO'S FIRST POSTULATE:

The good things in life also cause cancer in laboratory mice and are taxed beyond reality.

## CAPTAIN PENNY'S LAW:

You can fool all of the people some of the time, and some of the people all of the time, but you can't fool Mom.

## ISSAWI'S LAW OF THE CONSERVATION OF EVIL:

The total amount of evil in any system remains constant. Hence, any diminution in one direction — for instance, a reduction in poverty or unemployment — is accompanied by an increase in another, e.g., crime or air pollution.

## KATZ'S LAW:

Men and nations will act rationally when all other possibilities have been exhausted.

## PARKER'S LAW OF POLITICAL STATEMENTS:

The truth of any proposition has nothing to do with its credibility and vice versa.

## MR. COLE'S AXIOM:

The sum of the intelligence on the planet remains a constant; the population, however, continues to grow.

## LAW OF THE INDIVIDUAL:

Nobody really cares or understands what anyone else is doing.

## STEELE'S PLAGIARISM OF SOMEBODY'S PHILOSOPHY:

Everybody should believe in something — I believe I'll have another drink.

## McCLAUGHRY'S CODICIL TO JONES' MOTTO:

To make an enemy, do someone a favor.

## CANADA BILL JONES' MOTTO:

It's morally wrong to allow suckers to keep their money.

## Supplement:

A Smith and Wesson beats four aces.

## LEVY'S LAW:

That segment of the community with which one has the greatest sympathy as a liberal inevitably turns out to be one of the most narrow-minded and bigoted segments of the community.

## Kelly's Reformation:

Nice guys don't finish nice.

## THE KENNEDY CONSTANT:

Don't get mad — get even.

## JONES' MOTTO:

Friends come and go, but enemies accumulate.

## VIQUE'S LAW:

A man without religion is like a fish without a bicycle.

## THE FIFTH RULE:

You have taken yourself too seriously.

## SARTRE'S OBSERVATION:

Hell is others.

## DOOLEY'S LAW:

Trust everybody, but cut the cards.

## ZAPPA'S LAW:

There are two things on earth that are universal: hydrogen and stupidity.

## MUNDER'S THEOREM:

For every "10" there are ten "1s."

## DYKSTRA'S LAW:

Everybody is somebody else's weirdo.

## MEYERS' LAW:

In a social situation, that which is most difficult to do is usually the right thing to do.

## YOUNG'S PRINCIPLE OF EMERGENT INDIVIDUATION:

Everyone wants to peel his own banana.

## COHEN'S LAW:

People are divided into two groups—the righteous and the unrighteous—and the righteous do the dividing.

## THE IRE PRINCIPLE:

Never try to pacify people at the height of their rage.

## PYTHON'S PRINCIPLE OF TV MORALITY:

There is nothing wrong with sex on television, just as long as you don't fall off.

## KENT FAMILY LAW:

Never change your plans because of the weather.

## LIVINGSTON'S LAWS OF FAT:

1. Fat expands to fill any apparel worn.
2. A fat person walks in the middle of the hall.

   **Corollary:** Two fat people will walk side by side, whether they know each other or not.

## LAW OF ARRIVAL:

Those who live closest arrive latest.

## THE THREE LEAST CREDIBLE SENTENCES IN THE ENGLISH LANGUAGE:

1. "The check is in the mail."
2. "Of course I'll respect you in the morning."
3. "I'm from the government and I'm here to help you."

# MEDICAL
# MURPHOLOGY

# SIX PRINCIPLES FOR PATIENTS:

1. Just because your doctor has a name for your condition doesn't mean your doctor knows what it is.
2. The more boring and out-of-date the magazines in the waiting room, the longer you will have to wait for your scheduled appointment.
3. Only adults have difficulty with childproof bottles.
4. You never have the right number of pills left on the last day of a prescription.
5. The pills to be taken with meals will be the least appetizing ones.

   **Corollary:** Even water tastes bad when taken on doctor's orders.
6. If your condition seems to be getting better, it's probably your doctor getting sick.

# PARKINSON'S LAW FOR MEDICAL RESEARCH:

Successful research attracts the bigger grant, which makes further research impossible.

## MATZ'S WARNING:

Beware of the physician who is great at getting out of trouble.

## MATZ'S RULE REGARDING MEDICATIONS:

A drug is that substance which, when injected into a rat, will produce a scientific report.

## COCHRANE'S APHORISM:

Before ordering a test decide what you will do if it is 1) positive, or 2) negative. If both answers are the same, don't do the test.

## EDDS' LAW OF RADIOLOGY:

The colder the X-ray table, the more of your body you are required to place on it.

## BERNSTEIN'S PRECEPT:

The radiologists' national flower is the hedge.

## LORD COHEN'S COMMENT:

The feasibility of an operation is not the best indication for its performance.

# TELESCO'S LAWS OF NURSING:

1. All the IVs are at the other end of the hall.
2. A physician's ability is inversely proportional to his or her availability.
3. There are two kinds of adhesive tape: that which won't stay on and that which won't come off.
4. Everybody wants a pain shot at the same time.
5. Everybody who didn't want a pain shot when you were passing out pain shots wants one when you are passing out sleeping pills.

# BARACH'S RULE:

An alcoholic is a person who drinks more than his own physician.

# SPORTSMANSHIP-
# MANSHIP

## WISE FAN'S LAMENT:

Fools rush in — and get the best seats.

## BREDA'S RULE:

At any event, the people whose seats are farthest from the aisle arrive last.

## MOSER'S LAW OF SPECTATOR SPORTS:

Exciting plays occur only while you are watching the scoreboard or out buying a hot dog.

## BOB'S LAW OF TELEVISED SPORTS:

If you switch from one football game to another in order to avoid a commercial, the second game will be running a commercial too.

## MURRAY'S RULES OF THE ARENA:

1. Nothing is ever so bad it can't be made worse by firing the coach.
2. The wrong quarterback is the one that's in there.
3. A free agent is anything but.
4. Hockey is a game played by six good players and the home team.
5. Whatever can go to New York will.

## INDISPUTABLE LAW
## OF SPORTS CONTRACTS:

The more money the free agent signs for, the less effective he is the following season.

## KNOX'S PRINCIPLE OF STAR QUALITY:

Whenever a superstar is traded to your favorite team, he fades. Whenever your team trades away a useless no-name, he immediately rises to stardom.

## HERTZBERG'S LAW OF WING WALKING:

Never leave hold of what you've got until you've got hold of something else.

## TERMAN'S LAW OF INNOVATION:

If you want a track team to win the high jump, you find one person who can jump seven feet, not seven people who can jump one foot.

## LAVIA'S LAW OF TENNIS:

A mediocre player will sink to the level of his opposition.

## LEFTY GOMEZ'S LAW:

If you don't throw it, they can't hit it.

## LAW OF PRACTICE:

Plays that work in theory do not work in practice. Plays that work in practice do not work during the game.

## SIGSTAD'S LAW:

When it gets to be your turn, they change the rules.

## THE POKER PRINCIPLE:

Never do card tricks for the group you play poker with.

## STENDERUP'S LAW:

The sooner you fall behind, the more time you will have to catch up.

## WAGNER'S LAW OF SPORTS COVERAGE:

When the camera isolates on a male athlete, he will spit, pick or scratch.

## DEAL'S LAW OF SAILING:

1. The amount of wind will vary inversely with the number and experience of the people you take on board.
2. No matter how strong the breeze when you leave the dock, once you have reached the farthest point from the port, the wind will die.

## DORR'S LAW OF ATHLETICS:

In an otherwise empty locker room, any two individuals will have adjoining lockers.

# THE RULE OF THE RALLY:

The only way to make up for being lost is to make record time while you are lost.

# PORKINGHAM'S LAWS OF SPORTFISHING:

1. The time available to go fishing shrinks as the fishing season draws nearer.
2. The least experienced fisherman always catches the biggest fish.

   **Corollary:** The more elaborate and costly the equipment, the greater the chance of having to stop at the fish market on the way home.
3. The worse your line is tangled, the better the fishing is around you.

# MICHEHL'S RULE FOR PROSPECTIVE MOUNTAIN CLIMBERS:

The mountain gets steeper as you get closer.

## Frothingham's Corollary:

The mountain looks closer than it is.

## SHEDENHELM'S LAW OF BACKPACKING:

All trails have more uphill sections than they have level or downhill sections.

## LAW OF BRIDGE:

It's always the partner's fault.

## SMITH'S LAWS OF BRIDGE:

1. If your hand contains a singleton or a void, that is the suit your partner will bid.
2. If your hand contains the King, Jack , 9 of diamonds and the Ace of spades, when the dummy is spread to your left it will contain the Ace, Queen, 10 of diamonds and the King of spades.
3. The trump suit never breaks favorably when you are the declarer.

## THOMAS' LAW:

The one who least wants to play is the one who will win.

## HENRY'S QUIRK OF HUMAN NATURE:

Nobody loves a winner who wins all the time.

## TODD'S LAW:

All things being equal, you lose.

## Corollary:

All things being in your favor, you still lose.

## JENSEN'S LAW:

Win or lose, you lose.

# ROADSMANSHIP

## OLIVER'S LAW OF LOCATION:

No matter where you go, there you are!

## FIRST LAW OF TRAVEL:

It always takes longer to get there than to get back.

## THE AIRPLANE LAW:

When the plane you are on is late, the plane you want to transfer to is on time.

## LAW OF PROMOTIONAL TOURS:

Jet lag accumulates unidirectionally toward maximum difficulty to perform.

## STITZER'S VACATION PRINCIPLE:

When packing for a vacation, take half as much clothing and twice as much money.

## SNIDER'S LAW:

Nothing can be done in one trip.

## LAW OF BICYCLING:

No matter which way you ride, it's uphill and against the wind.

## HUMPHRIES' LAW OF BICYCLING:

The shortest route has the steepest hills.

## KELLY'S LAW OF AERIAL NAVIGATION:

The most important information on any chart is on the fold.

## GRANDPA CHARNOCK'S LAW:

You never really learn to swear until you learn to drive.

## VILE'S LAW OF ROADSMANSHIP:

Your own car uses more gas and oil than anyone else's.

## GRELB'S REMINDER:

Eighty percent of all people consider themselves to be above-average drivers.

## PHILLIPS' LAW:

Four-wheel drive just means getting stuck in more inaccessible places.

## LAW OF LIFE'S HIGHWAY:

If everything is coming your way, you're in the wrong lane.

# RELATIVITY FOR CHILDREN:

Time moves slower in a fast-moving vehicle.

# ATHENA'S RULES OF DRIVING COURTESY:

If you allow someone to get in front of you, either:

a) the car in front will be the last one over a railroad crossing, and you will be stuck waiting for a long, slow-moving train; or

b) you both will have the same destination, and the other car will get the last parking space.

# LEMAR'S PARKING POSTULATE:

If you have to park six blocks away, you will find two new parking spaces right in front of the building entrance.

# KARINTHY'S DEFINITION:

A bus is a vehicle that goes on the other side in the opposite direction.

# McKEE'S LAW:

When you're not in a hurry, the traffic light will turn green as soon as your vehicle comes to a complete stop.

## GRAY'S LAW FOR BUSES:

A bus that has refused to arrive will do so only when the would-be rider has walked to a point so close to the destination that it is no longer worthwhile to board the bus.

## QUIGLEY'S LAW:

A car and a truck approaching each other on an otherwise deserted road will meet at the narrow bridge.

## FIRST LAW OF TRAFFIC:

The slow lane you were stopped in starts moving as soon as you leave it.

## SECOND LAW OF TRAFFIC:

The extra hour you allowed for traffic will be superseded by an hour-and-a-half traffic jam.

## REECE'S LAW:

The speed of an oncoming vehicle is directly proportional to the length of the passing zone.

## MILLER'S LAW OF INSURANCE:

Insurance covers everything except what happens.

## MILSTEAD'S DRIVING PRINCIPLE:

Whenever you need to stop at a light to put on makeup, every light will be green.

## LOVKA'S LAW OF DRIVING:

There is no traffic until you need to make a left turn.

## DREW'S LAW OF HIGHWAY BIOLOGY:

The first bug to hit a clean windshield lands directly in front of your eyes.

## LAW OF HIGHWAY CONSTRUCTION:

The most heavily traveled streets spend the most time under construction.

## WINFIELD'S DICTUM OF DIRECTION GIVING:

The possibility of getting lost is directly proportional to the number of times the direction-giver says, "You can't miss it."

## JEAN'S LAW OF AUTOMOTIVES:

Any car utilized as a "back-up" car breaks down just after the primary car breaks down.

## CAMPBELL'S LAWS OF AUTOMOTIVE REPAIR:

1. If you can get to the faulty part, you don't have the tool to get it off.
2. If you can get the part off, the parts house will have it back-ordered.
3. If it's in stock, it didn't need replacing in the first place.

## BROMBERG'S LAWS
## OF AUTOMOTIVE REPAIR:

1. When the need arises, any tool or object closest to you becomes a hammer.
2. No matter how minor the task, you will inevitably end up covered with grease and motor oil.
3. When necessary, metric and inch tools can be used interchangeably.

## FEMO'S LAW OF
## AUTOMOTIVE ENGINE REPAIRING:

If you drop something, it will never reach the ground.

# HOUSEHOLD MURPHOLOGY

## O'REILLY'S LAW OF THE KITCHEN:

Cleanliness is next to impossible.

## ALICE HAMMOND'S LAWS OF THE KITCHEN:

1. Souffles rise and cream whips only for the family and for guests you didn't really want to invite anyway.
2. The rotten egg will be the one you break into the cake batter.
3. Any cooking utensil placed in the dishwasher will be needed immediately thereafter for something else; any measuring utensil used for liquid ingredients will be needed immediately thereafter for dry ingredients.
4. Time spent consuming a meal is in inverse proportion to time spent preparing it.
5. Whatever it is, somebody will have had it for lunch.

## THE PARTY LAW:

The more food you prepare, the less your guests eat.

## SEVEN LAWS OF KITCHEN CONFUSION:

1. Multiple-function gadgets will not perform any function adequately.

   **Corollary:** The more expensive the gadget, the less often you will use it.

2. The simpler the instructions (e.g., "Press here"), the more difficult it will be to open the package.

3. In a family recipe you just discovered in an old book, the most vital measurement will be illegible.

   **Corollary:** You will discover that you can't read it only after you have mixed all the other ingredients.

4. Once a dish is fouled up, anything added to save it only makes it worse.

5. You are always complimented on the item that took the least effort to prepare.

   **Example:** If you make "duck à l'orange," you will be complimented on the baked potato.

6. The one ingredient you made a special trip to the store to get will be the one thing your guest is allergic to.

7. The more time and energy you put into

preparing a meal, the greater the chance your guests will spend the entire meal discussing other meals they have had.

## WORKING COOK'S LAWS:

1. If you're wondering if you took the meat out to thaw, you didn't.
2. If you're wondering if you left the coffee pot plugged in, you did.
3. If you're wondering if you need to stop and pick up bread and eggs on the way home, you do.
4. If you're wondering if you have enough money to take the family out to eat tonight, you don't.

## MRS. WEILER'S LAW:

Anything is edible if it is chopped finely enough.

## FAUSNER'S RULE OF THE HOUSEHOLD:

A knife too dull to cut anything else can always cut your finger.

## FAUSNER'S DEFINITION:

Housework is what nobody notices unless it's not done.

## HAMILTON'S RULE FOR CLEANING GLASSWARE:

The spot you are scrubbing is always on the other side.

### Corollary:

If the spot is on the inside, you won't be able to reach it.

## YEAGER'S LAW:

Washing machines only break down during the wash cycle.

### Corollaries:

1. All breakdowns occur on the plumber's day off.
2. Cost of repair can be determined by multiplying the cost of your new coat by 1.75, or by multiplying the cost of a new washer by .75.

## WALKER'S LAW OF THE HOUSEHOLD:

There is always more dirty laundry than clean laundry.

### Clive's Rebuttal to Walker's Law:

If it's clean, it isn't laundry.

## SKOFF'S LAW:
A child will not spill on a dirty floor.

## WITZLING'S LAWS OF PROGENY PERFORMANCE:
1. Any child who chatters nonstop at home will adamantly refuse to utter a word when requested to demonstrate for an audience.
2. Any shy, introverted child will choose a crowded public area to loudly demonstrate newly acquired vocabulary (damn, penis, etc.).

## O'TOOLE'S AXIOM:

One child is not enough, but two children are far too many.

## VAN ROY'S LAW:

An unbreakable toy is useful for breaking other toys.

## H. FISH'S LAWS OF ANIMAL BEHAVIOR:

1. The probability of a cat eating its dinner has absolutely nothing to do with the price of the food placed before it.
2. The probability that a household pet will raise a fuss to go in or out is directly proportional to the number and importance of your dinner guests.

## THE PET PRINCIPLE:

No matter which side of the door the dog or cat is on, it is the wrong side.

## RULE OF FELINE FRUSTRATION:

When your cat has fallen asleep on your lap and looks utterly content and adorable, you will suddenly have to go to the bathroom.

## BOREN'S LAW FOR CATS:
When in doubt, wash.

## FISKE'S TEENAGE COROLLARY TO PARKINSON'S LAW:
The stomach expands to accommodate the amount of junk food available.

## BANANA PRINCIPLE:
If you buy bananas or avocados before they are ripe, there won't be any left by the time they are ripe. If you buy them ripe, they rot before they are eaten.

## BALLANCE'S LAW OF RELATIVITY:
How long a minute is depends on which side of the bathroom door you're on.

## BRITT'S GREEN THUMB POSTULATE:
The life expectancy of a house plant varies inversely with its price and directly with its ugliness.

## MARQUETTE'S FIRST LAW OF HOME REPAIR:
The tool you need is just out of reach.

## MARQUETTE'S SECOND LAW OF HOME REPAIR:

The first replacement part you buy will be the wrong size.

## MARQUETTE'S THIRD LAW OF HOME REPAIR:

A lost tool will be found immediately upon purchasing a new one.

## MALONE'S LAW OF THE HOUSEHOLD:

If you wait all day for the repairman, you'll wait all day. If you go out for five minutes, he'll arrive and leave while you're gone.

## MINTON'S LAW OF PAINTING:

Any paint, no matter what the quality or composition, will adhere permanently to any surface if applied accidentally.

## LAWS OF GARDENING:

1. Other people's tools work only in other people's gardens.
2. Fancy gizmos don't work.
3. If nobody uses it, there's a reason.
4. You get the most of what you need the least.

## KITMAN'S LAW:

Pure drivel tends to drive ordinary drivel off the TV screen.

## LAW OF RERUNS:

If you have watched a TV series only once, and you watch it again, it will be a rerun of the same episode.

## JONES' LAW OF TV PROGRAMMING:

1. If there are only two shows worth watching, they will be on at the same time.
2. The only new show worth watching will be cancelled.
3. The show you've been looking forward to all week will be preempted.

## BESS' UNIVERSAL PRINCIPLES:

1. The telephone will ring when you are outside the door, fumbling for your keys.
2. You will reach it just in time to hear the click of the caller hanging up.

## KOVAC'S CONUNDRUM:

When you dial a wrong number, you never get a busy signal.

## BELL'S THEOREM:
When a body is immersed in water, the telephone rings.

## RYAN'S APPLICATION OF PARKINSON'S LAW:
Possessions increase to fill the space available for their storage.

## RINGWALD'S LAW OF HOUSEHOLD GEOMETRY:
Any horizontal surface is soon piled up.

## THE PINEAPPLE PRINCIPLE:
The best parts of anything are always impossible to separate from the inedible parts.

## LAW OF SUPERMARKETS:
The quality of the house brand varies inversely with the size of the supermarket chain.

## LAW OF SUPERMARKET SHOPPING:
The longer the shopping list, the more likely it will be left at home.

## THE GROCERY BAG LAW:

The candy bar you planned to eat on the way home from the market will be at the bottom of the grocery bag.

## WOODSIDE'S GROCERY PRINCIPLE:

The bag that breaks is the one with the eggs.

## ESTHER'S LAW:

The fussiest person will be the one to get the chipped coffee cup, the glass with lipstick or the hair in the food.

## POPE'S LAW:

Chipped dishes never break.

## HOROWITZ'S LAW:

Whenever you turn on the radio, you hear the last few notes of your favorite song.

## ZELMAN'S RULE OF RADIO RECEPTION:

Your pocket radio won't pick up the station you want to hear most.

## GERARD'S LAW:

When there are sufficient funds in the checking account, checks take two weeks to clear. When there are insufficient funds, checks clear overnight.

## SEYMOUR'S INVESTMENT PRINCIPLE:

Never invest in anything that eats.

# CONSUMEROLOGY
# AND
# SALESMANSHIP

## HERBLOCK'S LAW:

If it's good, they discontinue it.

## GOLD'S LAW:

If the shoe fits, it's ugly.

## HADLEY'S LAWS OF CLOTHING SHOPPING:

1. If you like it, they don't have it in your size.
2. If you like it and they have it in your size, it doesn't fit anyway.
3. If you like it and it fits, you can't afford it.
4. If you like it, it fits and you can afford it, it falls apart the first time you wear it.

## FINMAN'S BARGAIN BASEMENT PRINCIPLE:

The one you want is never the one on sale.

## Baker's Corollary:

You never want the one you can afford.

## LEWIS' LAW:

No matter how long or how hard you shop for an item, after you've bought it, it will be on sale somewhere cheaper.

## HERSHISER'S RULES:
1. Anything labeled "NEW" and/or "IMPROVED" isn't.
2. The label "NEW" and/or "IMPROVED" means the price went up.
3. The label "ALL NEW," "COMPLETELY NEW" or "GREAT NEW" means the price went way up.

## McGOWAN'S MADISON AVENUE AXIOM:
If an item is advertised as "under $50," you can bet it's not $19.95.

## LAW OF THE MARKETPLACE:
If only one price can be obtained for any quotation, the price will be unreasonable.

## SECOND LAW OF THE MARKETPLACE:
Weekend specials aren't.

## PANTUSO'S LAW:
The book you spent $10.95 for today will come out in paperback tomorrow.

## GLASER'S LAW:
If it says "one size fits all," it doesn't fit anyone.

## RILEY'S "MURPHY'S LAW" LAWS:

1. Stores that sell Volume One will not know of Volume Two.
2. Stores that sell Volume Two will be out of Volume One.

## VILE'S LAW OF VALUE:

The more an item costs, the farther you have to send it for repairs.

## MURRAY'S LAWS:

1. Never ask a barber if you need a haircut.
2. Never ask a salesman if his is a good price.

## GOLDENSTERN'S RULES:

1. Always hire a rich attorney.
2. Never buy from a rich salesperson.

## SINTETOS' LAW OF CONSUMERISM:

A sixty-day warranty guarantees that the product will self-destruct on the sixty-first day.

## BERYL'S LAW:

The *Consumer Report* article on the item will come out a week after you've made your purchase.

## Corollaries:

1. The one you bought will be rated "unacceptable."
2. The one you almost bought will be rated "best buy."

## SAVIGNANO'S MAIL-ORDER LAW:

If you don't write to complain, you'll never receive your order.

If you do write, you'll receive the merchandise before your angry letter reaches its destination.

## YOUNT'S LAWS OF MAIL ORDERING:

1. The most important item in an order will no longer be available.
2. The next most important item will be back-ordered for six months.
3. During the time an item is back-ordered, it will be available more cheaply and quickly from many other sources.
4. As soon as a back-order has entered the "no longer available" category, the item will no longer be obtainable anywhere at any price.

## LEWIS' LAW:

People will buy anything that's one to a customer.

# BROOKS' LAW OF RETAILING:

Security isn't.
Management can't.
Sales promotions don't.
Consumer assistance doesn't.
Workers won't.

# COSMO-MURPHOLOGY

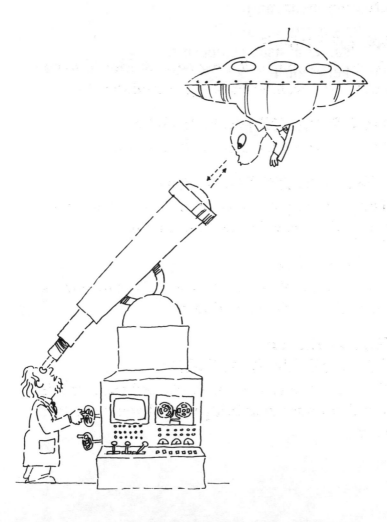

## OLIVIER'S LAW:

Experience is something you don't get until just after you need it.

## LAW OF LIVING:

As soon as you're doing what you wanted to be doing, you want to be doing something else.

## FIRST RULE OF PATHOLOGY:

Most well-trodden paths lead nowhere.

## GABITOL'S OBSERVATION:

The wise are pleased when they discover truth, fools when they discover falsehood.

## FOSTER'S LAW:

The only people who find what they are looking for in life are the fault-finders.

## FIRST RULE OF NEGATIVE ANTICIPATION:

You will save yourself a lot of needless worry if you don't burn your bridges until you come to them.

## FIRST PRINCIPLE OF SELF-DETERMINATION:

What you resist, you become.

## STEINER'S PRECEPTS:

1. Knowledge based on external evidence is unreliable.
2. Logic can never decide what is possible or impossible.

## COLRIDGE'S LAW:

Extremes meet.

## FEINBERG'S PRINCIPLE:

Memory serves its own master.

## VOLTAIRE'S LAW:

There is nothing more respectable than an ancient evil.

## LAST LAW OF ROBOTICS:

The only real errors are human errors.

## HOFFER'S LAW:

When people are free to do as they please, they usually imitate each other.

## BERRA'S FIRST LAW:
You can observe a lot just by watching.

## BERRA'S SECOND LAW:
Anyone who is popular is bound to be disliked.

## PERLSWEIG'S LAW:
Whatever goes around, comes around.

## MEADOW'S MAXIM:
You can't push on a rope.

## OPPENHEIMER'S LAW:
There is no such thing as instant experience.

## DISIMONI'S RULE OF COGNITION:
Believing is seeing.

## THE SIDDHARTHA PRINCIPLE:
You cannot cross a river in two strides.

## KIERKEGAARD'S OBSERVATION:
Life can only be understood backwards, but it must be lived forward.

# METALAWS

## LES MISERABLES METALAW:

All laws, whether good, bad or indifferent, must be obeyed to the letter.

## PERSIG'S POSTULATE:

The number of rational hypotheses that can explain any given phenomenon is infinite.

## LILLY'S METALAW:

All laws are simulations of reality.

## THE ULTIMATE PRINCIPLE:

By definition, when you are investigating the unknown you do not know what you will find.

## COOPER'S METALAW:

A proliferation of new laws creates a proliferation of new loopholes.

## DIGIOVANNI'S LAW:

The number of laws will expand to fill the publishing space available.

## LEO ROGERS' BLESSING FOR VOLUME II:

If it's worth doing, it's worth overdoing.

## ROGERS' OBSERVATION REGARDING THE LAWS:

In a bureaucratic hierarchy, the higher up in the organization you go, the less people appreciate Murphy's Law, the Peter Principle, etc.

## OAK'S PRINCIPLES OF LAW-MAKING:

1. Law expands in proportion to the resources available for its enforcement.
2. Bad law is more likely to be supplemented than repealed.
3. Social legislation cannot repeal physical laws.

## JAFFE'S PRECEPT:

There are some things that are impossible to know — but it is impossible to know these things.

## MUIR'S LAW:

When we try to pick out anything by itself, we find it hitched to everything else in the universe.

## MIKSCH'S LAW:

If a string has one end, then it has another end.

## COLE'S LAW:

Thinly sliced cabbage.

# DUCHARM'S AXIOM:

If one views one's problem closely enough, one will recognize oneself as part of the problem.

# LAW OF ARBITRARY DISTINCTION:

Anything may be divided into as many parts as you please.

## Corollary:

Everything may be divided into as many parts as you please.

## Commentary on the Corollary:

In this case, "everything" may be viewed as a subset of "anything."

# WALLACE'S OBSERVATION:

Everything is in a state of utter dishevelment.

# WELWOOD'S AXIOM:

Disorder expands proportionately to the tolerance for it.

# HARTLEY'S SECOND LAW:

You can lead a horse to water, but if you can get him to float on his back, you've got something.

## FOWLER'S NOTE:

The only imperfect thing in nature is the human race.

## TRISCHMANN'S PARADOX:

A pipe gives a wise man time to think and a fool something to stick in his mouth.

## CHURCHILL'S COMMENTARY ON MAN:

Man will occasionally stumble over the truth, but most of the time he will pick himself up and continue on.

## HALDANE'S LAW:

The universe is not only queerer than we imagine, it's queerer than we *can* imagine.

## LAW OF OBSERVATION:

Nothing looks as good close up as it does from far away.

Or — nothing looks as good from far away as it does close up.

## THE AQUINAS AXIOM:

What the gods get away with, the cows don't.

## NEWTON'S LITTLE-KNOWN SEVENTH LAW:

A bird in the hand is safer than one overhead.

## WHITE'S CHAPPAQUIDDICK THEOREM:

The sooner and in more detail you announce the bad news, the better.

## THE LAST LAW:

If several things that could have gone wrong have not gone wrong, it would have been ultimately beneficial for them to have gone wrong.

## MATSCH'S LAW:

It's better to have a horrible ending than to have horrors without end.